MENTA...
AND SCHIZOPHRENIA

The Nutrition Connection

MENTAL ILLNESS

AND SCHIZOPHRENIA

The Nutrition Connection

How orthomolecular therapy can correct body chemistry
imbalance without side-effects

Dr CARL C. PFEIFFER (Edited by Patrick Holford B.Sc.)

THORSONS PUBLISHING GROUP LIMITED
Wellingborough, Northamptonshire
Rochester, Vermont

First published in the United Kingdom 1987

British Library Cataloguing in Publication Data

Pfeiffer, Carl C.
Mental illness and schizophrenia: the nutritional connection.
1. Schizophrenia—Diet therapy
I. Title   II. Holford, Patrick
616.89'820654   RC514

ISBN 0-7225-1465-4

Printed and bound in Great Britain

Acknowledgements

The author acknowledges the expert help of Marie Arcaro BA, Elizabeth Jenny MS and Dr Eric Braverman MD in the preparation of this book. This book was made possible by a gift from the Thomas M. Peters Trust and the support of my publishers, Thorsons.

This book is dedicated to

The many patients who have died or are mentally crippled because of lack of nutritional treatment.

The many more who presently are denied effective nutritional therapy in our mental hospitals.

The few who have been lost by the staff of the Brain Bio Center because our nutritional knowledge had not matured.

Contents

Note to Reader

Preface

There are few people in the world today who have had the experience of working with so many mentally ill people as Dr Carl Pfeiffer. At the age of 23 as a young medical student he first became aware that nutrition might have something to do with mental function. Having qualified, he fast became recognized as a leading light in America in research into schizophrenia. After 28 years in psychiatric research, he suffered a severe heart attack when he was 51. This event made him realize just how important nutrition is to us all and intensified his research into nutrition and mental illness. Now 69 years of age, he is still hard at work on these researches. He is the author of five books: *The Schizophrenias – Yours and Mine* (1970): *Mental and Elemental Nutrients* (1975): *The Factbook on Zinc and Other Micronutrients* (1978): *Dr Pfeiffer's Total Nutrition* (1980): and *The Golden Pamphlet* (1980), selling more than 150,000 copies worldwide. Since 1937 Dr Pfeiffer and his research team have had published more than 300 scientific research papers in leading journals throughout the world.

His team consists of thirty-five employees (seven of them scientists) with himself as Director of the Brain Bio Center, the leading research centre into mental illness and nutrition in the world.

About the Brain Bio Center
The Brain Bio Center is a non-profit making, out-patient clinic and research centre in New Jersey, USA, under the auspices of the

Schizophrenia Foundation of New Jersey and the New Jersey Mental Health Development Research Fund. The Brain Bio Center continues the work of the Bureau of Research in Neurology and Psychiatry (previously part of the New Jersey Psychiatric Institute) which was closed in 1973 by the state because of lack of funds. During a period of thirteen years at the Bureau, biochemical tests for the identification of various types of schizophrenia were developed. These tests continue to be refined and extended.

Research into Histamine levels

One of these was an accurate method for the determination of blood levels of the important brain chemical, histamine. This led to the discovery that blood histamine levels were much lower in a group of patients suffering from one type of schizophrenia than in others. After treatment with an effective drug, the histamine level rose to normal as the patients improved. Further examination of schizophrenic patients showed a different group with very high histamine levels.

The copper connection

Other studies involved the determination of trace element levels in the blood of patients. High copper levels were found in adults with depression, as well as in hyperactive children. Low zinc levels were found in patients with the 'mauve factor' in their urine samples. (Earlier it had been discovered that a higher proportion of schizophrenics had a strange 'mauve factor' in their urine. This has since been identified as the presence of pyrroles.) Research revealed that this was because 'pyroluric' patients excreted more zinc than usual. Since 1971 Dr Carl Pfeiffer and his team have studied several thousand pyroluric patients. In 1973 they discovered that untreated pyroluric patients had little or no dream recall. When given adequate amounts of zinc, vitamin B_6 and manganese, not only did dream recall usually improve but so did their mental illness.

The Brain Bio Center – past and present

With the move away from the New Jersey Psychiatric Institute, the new Brain Bio Center broadened its field of interest. It was no longer limited to the study of the schizophrenias and is currently actively engaged in the study of many disorders including hypoglycaemia (low blood sugar), arthritis, colds, herpes, allergic and digestive disorders, as well as heavy metal poisoning due to mercury, cadmium, bismuth, lead, berylium and copper.

From 1973 to 1981 the Brain Bio Center was located in the rear of a shopping centre, a rather drab setting. But demand for treatment from people all over the world led to the need for a proper centre. Money was raised during a period of five years and a new building with unequalled facilities for research, diagnosis and treatment was opened in 1981.

With the new Brain Bio Center came an expanded team of twelve doctors, researchers, nurses and nutritionists and an ever-expanding list of research achievements that are pushing the treatment of mental illness, and other disorders, into a new era. But perhaps the Brain Bio Center's most important contribution is that of education and dissemination of these new and vitally important discoveries.

The education side of the Center's work is helped by the Schizophrenia Foundation of New Jersey. This is a voluntary association of lay-people, doctors, and scientists which was organized in 1967. More than 450 members help by means of membership fees, gifts, and the sale of publications. The major contribution of the Foundation is to help people realize that mental disorders are common, that early recognition of the symptoms will lead to earlier recovery, and that patients and relatives should be encouraged by the knowledge that such illness can be treated successfully.

Foreword

The Chinese have a saying 'Disease enters through the mouth'. Yet it appears that many doctors do not like this concept. To consider food as contributing to the development of disease is often thought to be unorthodox and alternative.

The critics seem particularly unable to consider that certain foods could produce mental illness. They think schizophrenia is confined to the brain. How, then, could this important and isolated organ be affected by the nutrition of the body? Yet, of course, the brain is entirely dependent on adequate and suitable nutrition.

Remarkably, Dr Carl Pfeiffer has decided to examine the biochemistry of his psychotic patients. He has found high or low levels of nutrients and other body chemicals and, where possible, he has normalized them. He has tested for food sensitivities and blood sugar levels. He has measured histamine levels and urine pyrrole levels. Above all he has observed his patients. He has asked them about themselves. He has learned about their special problems. He has then grouped his patients into (often overlapping) groups according to symptomatology and devised nutritional therapies for them according to observation and biochemical profile.

So few psychiatrists think these days to ask their patients about their physical symptoms. They still too often concentrate on family relationships as being causative or contributory to the appearance of psychiatric symptoms. Long ago, psychiatrists sought the physical symptoms that were at the root of the trouble.

They considered the interaction of diet as Dr Pfeiffer does now. Carl Pfeiffer's book *Mental Illness and Schizophrenia – The Nutrition Connection* offers hope to many and gives information on how patients can begin to improve their own health through nutrition and proper medication. Health is something to be greatly desired by the ill and they need to be taught how to help themselves. We do not know how many mentally ill people could be helped by methods described in this book, but it is worth every psychiatric patient finding out if he can use it to improve his health.

We need psychiatrists to take up nutrition as part of their weaponry against disease. If they follow Carl Pfeiffer's leads, they will be a good step along the way of helping their patients to get a lot better than many who are now on drug treatment alone.

Gwynneth Hemmings
Honorary Secretary of the Schizophrenia Association of Great Britain, 1987

1

Mental Illness – Not All in the Mind

One in a hundred people is diagnosed as suffering from schizophrenia. Many more suffer from depression, anxiety, extreme fears and phobias. For some this is controllable just by avoiding stressful situations, but for others help is badly needed. But what treatment is available? For the seriously mentally ill this means psychiatric help. Some psychiatrists view mental illness as a psychologically based disease, a perplexing nightmare often intertwined with suspicious family interactions. The treatment may be endless psychoanalysis and an endless drain on financial resources with little more than a slim chance of help. (As one patient said after years of psychoanalysis, 'I may know myself a lot better but I'm still mentally ill!') Other psychiatrists lean more heavily on drug treatments, but these too have only a small chance of really helping. Many psychotherapeutic drugs leave the patient drowsy and 'drugged' and have nasty side-effects (for which other drugs have to be given) as well as carrying the risk of brain damage. There was no alternative until recently!

The 'Orthomolecular' approach
The term 'orthomolecular' was first coined by Nobel Prize winner Linus Pauling to give a word to the treatment of disease with nutrients. Ortho means 'right' so orthomolecular simply means supplying your cells with the right mix of nutrients. Since many diseases are known to be the result of the body getting the wrong balance of essential nutrients by adjusting diet, eliminating junk foods, and ingesting large doses of essential vitamins, minerals and

trace metals, amino acids and polyunsaturated fats, the chemical imbalances of disease can be corrected. 'Mega vitamin therapy' was first coined in 1952 by psychiatrists Humphrey Osmond and Abram Hoffer to describe the large dosages of niacin (vitamin B_3) used in the treatment of schizophrenic, LSD and amphetamine psychosis. 'Mega vitamin' therapy, better called 'meganutrient', has become a part of orthomolecular medicine which has

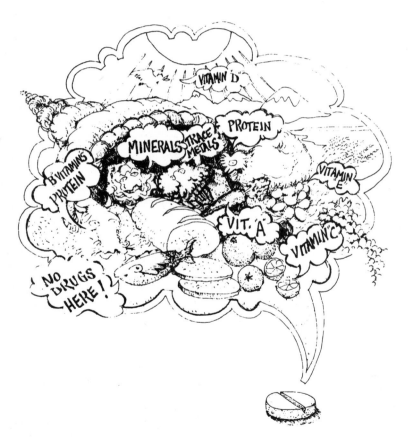

Figure 1. Vitamin and mineral tablets contain no drugs, only nutrients.

continually expanded and now recognizes that all of man's biological interactions with food, water, air and light are an important part of good health and the prevention of illness if they are obtained in the right amounts.

For example, cadmium-polluted air contributes to high blood pressure and hardening of the arteries; fluorescent lighting can cause hyperactivity; aluminium-rich drinking water causes aluminium poisoning which may cause senility; copper plumbing results in copper overload disorders such as hypertension; high sugar intake contributes to hypoglycaemia, diabetes and heart disease; and food additives may cause allergies, particularly in children.

The orthomolecular approach also helps patients become more aware of our dangerously polluted environment and nutrient-stripped, refined foods. Proper diet and nutritional supplements can protect us from the harmful effects of lead, cadmium and mercury. Orthomolecular therapy is therefore both corrective and preventive.

Orthomolecular medicine today is primarily used in the treatment of psychiatric disorders and orthomolecular psychiatrists make up approximately 1 per cent of the 30,000 practising psychiatrists in America and less than 0.1 per cent of psychiatrists in Britain and other European countries.

The scope of treatable disorders has continually broadened since the initial treatment of schizophrenics, to include epilepsy, autism, senility, childhood hyperactivity, arthritis, colds, herpes simplex virus, and allergic and digestive problems, to name but a few. For instance, arthritis which limits the use of joints responds to zinc supplementation and so does the worry associated with the condition. The doctors who treat these diseases are practising orthomolecular medicine, but sadly the nutritionally-orientated medical practitioner is a rare bird.

The type of treatment offered by orthomolecular doctors varies but the main stream of work focuses upon meganutrient therapy after careful diagnostic tests. Treatment with adequate nutrients is the distinguishing therapy of orthomolecular medicine. The rationale for treatment is arrived at through a variety of clinical tests, psychiatric examinations, and consultations. Trained doctors interpreting these tests recognize the biochemical individuality of each patient. That is, each patient may have very different nutrient requirements.

Because orthomolecular treatments often take months to achieve the best results, the use of meganutrients is not highly regarded among practising doctors as being useful in the treatment of pain, insomnia, headaches and acute depression, for example. Orthodox treatment for these symptoms is usually with pain-killers, sleeping pills, psychotherapy or even electric-shock therapy, all of which are effective but not curative. While it is becoming widely recognized that orthomolecular therapy cures patients by correcting body chemistry imbalances, it is little known that, in certain combinations, meganutrients can be as immediately effective as potent pain-killers or tranquillizers. Vitamin C and niacin (B_3) (in dosages that provide a mild blushing sensation) provide almost instant relief to the overactive mind, and help focus mental concentration. Vitamin B_6 with zinc and manganese is particularly effective in relieving the symptoms of low blood sugar. These treatments have no long-term or immediate adverse reactions, compared to aspirin, which may eat away your stomach lining, or tranquillizers which bring on a grotesque tremor that mimics Parkinson's disease, called tardive dyskinesia.

Meganutrients treat both the immediate and the long-term cause of the disease, and disease, while it may have a sudden onset, is usually rooted in our past dietary and physical indiscretions. Since meganutrient therapy treats the whole person's biochemical imbalances, it can be of immediate and long-term benefit. There is no justification for the use of drugs except in the case of the critically ill. Generally, the use of drugs is a self-deception which sacrifices long-term health for immediate results. If meganutrients are not entirely effective, vigorous exercise will almost always restore the bodily equilibrium and homeostasis.

In the past decade, orthomolecular doctors and nutritionists

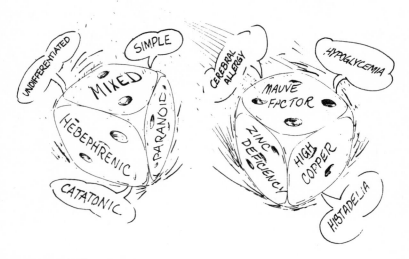

Figure 2. Let's role both dice for the schizophrenias.

have expanded their use of special diets. Hypoglycaemia (low blood sugar), found in many mentally ill patients suffering from chronic ailments, has resulted in the standardization of the high vegetable protein, low refined carbohydrate, no junk food diet. The discovery that food additives, artificial colours, flavours and preservatives can cause hyperactivity in children and 'brain' allergy in adults, has resulted in the use of more natural diets.

In addition, orthomolecular doctors have discovered that both patients and normal people may have an allergy to one or more of the nutritious foods which modern society serves in almost constant repetition. These include milk, eggs, beef, wheat and corn products.

This finding is hardly new, since Lucretius wrote 2,000 years ago: 'What is one man's meat is another man's poison'. Thus, careful allergy testing, desensitization, rotation of foods over a four-day period, food elimination diets and periods of fasting are all useful tools of the orthomolecular doctor.

Susceptibility to allergies and exposure to additives as part of a nutritionally derelict diet contribute to any individual becoming susceptible to the stresses of everyday life. With an optimum diet one can reduce the need for using such large doses of nutrients to restore good health.

Ideally, orthomolecular medicine teaches practitioners and patients an awareness of their reactions to the environment and their individual needs. Good living, regular exercise, relaxation, and a natural diet, preferably in a clean environment, are essential parts of any holistic therapy.

2

Understanding Mental Illness

So you think you have something wrong with your mind. It's playing tricks on you! Your view of the world and your friends has somehow changed. You may feel depressed, find yourself reacting out of proportion, feel useless, flat and put upon! You can't smile when it's appropriate to smile. You may feel too high, excited and even grandiose. You can't sleep. How long can you go on like this?

You may feel suspicious of all around you, including your loved ones. Does Mum's aspirin bottle really contain aspirin? Maybe not! It didn't stop your headache. Does that flashing electric sign outside your window give coded messages of your thoughts to the world? Has the CIA removed your parents and put imposters in their place? What about all those electrical waves that come through the walls to make your radio and television work?

You calculate that this abnormal disperceptive state could come from outside or inside. The outside factors may be the phases of the moon, the phases of the planets (Jupiter effect), sun spots, the abnormal winds, the bright sun, the continued rain or fog, the continued hot or cold spell, your exposure to heavy metals or street drugs, to list but a few.

The internal causes could be your menstrual cycle, your over-indulgence in food or drink, your daily six cups of coffee, your failure to get your morning cup of coffee, going too long without food, that late, late show, your lack of exercise, or a host of other internal psychic or physical factors. Obviously, some are controllable and some are not.

The wise therapist will help you sort out all these external and internal factors in order to provide relief for your disperceptions. Sometimes reassurance by the therapist is all that is needed since the outside or internal cause of the mental quirk may disappear within days.

If the feeling of abnormal elation, depression or unreality does not disappear with proper food and a good night's sleep, then appropriate action must be taken since nothing is worse than the speculation that something is wrong with your mind and senses. Your normal sensory input and mental balance with a good memory is your identity. If you cannot remember your past, cannot deal with the present and cannot plan for the future, then you are indeed mentally ill. Abnormal brain function with disperceptions is the ultimate threat which can lead to total destruction of both body and mind.

Several main types of natural mental illness occur which may cause disperceptions. The schizophrenias make up the class which is most severe, the most widespread and the greatest cause of hospitalization. Even when used in the plural, the term schizophrenia is an inadequate and misleading diagnosis. 'Disperceptions of unknown cause' is a better term.

The main biotypes of the schizophrenias are five in number. These are:

1. Histapenia – low blood histamine with excess copper: 50 per cent of the schizophrenias.

2. Histadelia – high blood histamine with low copper: 20 per cent of the schizophrenias.

3. Pyroluria – a familial double deficiency of zinc and vitamin B_6: 30 per cent of the schizophrenias.

4. Cerebral allergy – includes wheat-gluten allergy: 10 per cent of the schizophrenias.

5. Nutritional hypoglycaemia: 20 per cent of the schizophrenias.

These percentages do not add up to exactly 100 per cent because many patients have more than one disorder. In our out-patient clinic (The Princeton Brain Bio Center) we have treated over 5,000 patients labelled schizophrenic. Of these, 95 per cent can be categorized into the five types described above. When the exact biotype guides the appropriate treatment, 90 per cent of these patients will attain social rehabilitation.

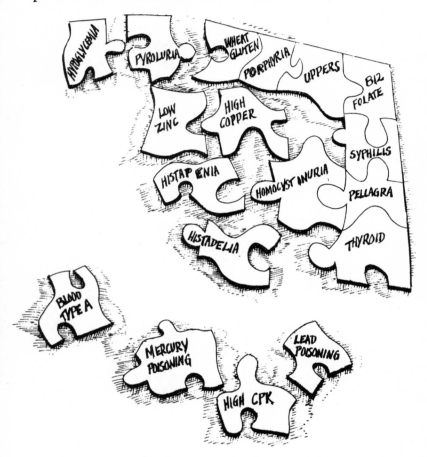

Figure 3. The jigsaw pieces of the puzzle of the schizophrenias.

Understanding schizophrenia

There are many conflicting descriptions and explanations for the schizophrenias, but at a basic level, there is usually little difficulty in making a preliminary diagnosis; and there is usually agreement among doctors in making the diagnosis, even though they may disagree about the possible causes and the ultimate outcome for any given patient. Since the schizophrenias may vary from simple (but abnormal) feelings of disperception or persecution to complete loss of contact with reality, the doctor hesitates to apply the term schizophrenia to the mild forms of disorder. Instead he uses the terms 'schizoid personality', 'schizophrenic reaction', or other such words. The doctor really means 'I am puzzled and will sit on the fence until I see what happens to you in the next year or so as you freewheel through life with or without medication'.

Uniform features of the schizophrenias on which doctors agree, are that disorders of thought, perception and experience or interaction occur. The schizophrenias are a subjective or personal mental aberration, with no clear or reliable external manifestations. A broken bone would be easier to bear, because it is objective and obviously real. The lack of firm, objective signs is perhaps the crux of the continuing argument as to whether the schizophrenias may have any physiological or biochemical basis.

Some of the schizophrenias can be likened to a nightmare state from which there is no certain awakening. Even more accurately, the experiences of schizophrenics are reproduced in certain toxic or feverous states. The normal person on recovery from a high fever with delusions, can breathe a great sigh of relief at the thought that his experience was temporary and will not occur again. The person under the influence of the hallucinogenic drug LSD has the clock as his best friend, since the drug-induced schizophrenia will wear off with time. For the person with the worst kind of the schizophrenias, however, the abnormal state has no let up and may be a continuing nightmare.

What divides abnormal behaviour from mental illness?
A valid point for debate is whether certain abnormal behaviour qualifies as mental illness. Patients who have certain mental symptoms after strokes or infections of the brain present no

problem in being considered ill. In contrast, there is a group of disorders listed, in the standard nomenclature of the American Psychiatric Association, as 'character and behaviour disorders'. There is nothing in these terms to suggest any organic or physiological derangement, so to call them mental illness, although currently fashionable, is stretching the term considerably.

Manic-depression

Somewhere between these extremes are patients with two major psychoses: the schizophrenias and manic-depressive psychosis. It has become popular also to regard manic-depressive psychosis as 'better' than schizophrenia. Manic-depressive psychosis has long been felt to have a biochemical basis, and anyway, doctors claim 'it is only a disorder of emotions, the patient isn't really crazy'. Perhaps this is, in part, because intellectual functioning may be less impaired than in one of the severe schizophrenias.

Schizophrenia has become a dirty word, a diagnosis to be whispered, and often to be concealed from patient, family, or friends. Again, a broken leg or even blindness would be more bearable, because it is visible, explicable, and being plainly physical, is something one can live with. Socially determined bias has a role in the way the two kinds of major mental disease are regarded. In a way, to be depressed is noble. Kings and even Abraham Lincoln had spells of depression. 'To be good you must suffer' is stated in many religions.

Yet the schizophrenias, about which some people have such strong and irrational feelings (no doubt because of their own fears or other emotional reactions), strike everywhere throughout all of mankind. The commonly quoted figure of 1 per cent of all humanity is probably far short of the actual incidence. We should add to this estimate the walking wounded who are never seen by any doctor, since only one-third of those afflicted need be hospitalized. We must also add the teenager who commits suicide before an accurate diagnosis is made. Thus the problem is one which is important from the viewpoint of numbers, as well as individual misery. Heart disease may cause more deaths, but the schizophrenias cause more heart-ache. Given a choice, most of us who have tasted adult freedom would prefer a quick death rather than the aimless custody of any mental institution, which may be the fate of the untreated schizophrenic.

Understanding paranoia

What brings the patient and doctor together? The things which characterize the untreated schizophrenias can be separated into two classes: those which bother the patient and those which bother those around the patient. The two botherations may not be the same. In fact, there is often considerable friction between the patient and others. Consider the case of the man who says he has visions and hears the voice of Jesus. Hallucinations are considered by doctors to be evidence of psychosis; but what if this man is a lay preacher to one of the churches which teach that if you only have enough faith, Christ will appear in person? To him then, the people who say he is mentally ill are merely a bunch of non-believers. The preacher is an example of the fact that leadership and secondary gain frequently go with the delusions and hallucinations of many paranoids. Many of the stresses and frustrations of everyday life could be assuaged if one had a firm belief in being a chosen child or disciple of God (many people have this without being delusional about it, of course).

This discord creates certain practical difficulties. Consider the case of a paranoid young woman. She keeps insisting to her family that she is carrying the new Christ-child in her abdomen because she hasn't had a menstrual period for three months. This lack of a menstrual period is usually owing to a lack of zinc in her body because of stress and eating a zinc deficient diet high in refined sugar. The family is upset and annoyed by her continued delusion as well as by her untidiness, lack of co-operation and general unpleasantness around the house. Complaints are then made to the family doctor, but by the family, not by the patient. The patient refuses flatly to even talk to the doctor, insisting that she is in good health: 'It's just that my family don't understand me and my new role in society.' This kind of situation can create a dilemma for the doctor. Although the diagnosis is reasonably clear, should the doctor insist on treating a patient who has not asked for help? Of course, if the patient asks for treatment there is no problem. If the patient presents some clear evidence that he or she may harm someone, intervention is clearly justified. However, aside from the unethical taint of unsolicited treatment, a major goal is to keep patients out of the hospitals whenever possible. Sometimes that alone is a victory, because with some of our present mental hospitals, there is the probability that the patient may be better off at home. One situation that creates great difficulty occurs when the doctor suspects that the patient may be suicidal or homicidal. Since the conservation of human life has high priority, the physician must try to treat the patient. Being only human and acting on the basis of insufficient tests, the doctor is sometimes wrong, no matter how great his ability. Patients, after such a false alarm, are often bitter and unforgiving. Indeed, they frequently incorporate the memory of such a forced hospitalization into their delusional systems.

Causes of Schizophrenia
The five main types of schizophrenia and their causes were listed on page 24. But can schizophrenias really be defined as simply as that? Can life or individuals be categorized that easily? No, indeed! The fact is that if we include fevers, environmental pains and drug reactions, there must be a hundred ways to go crazy and be diagnosed as schizophrenic. Our patients realize that we are carefully sorting out the different causes of their craziness and they are usually tolerant of any mistakes since we are doing everything we can to get at the root cause of their illness.

A more comprehensive list of possible causes for disperceptions that cause schizophrenia is shown in the table below. The chapters which follow explain many of these major types, how to identify them and, most important of all, how nutrition can help correct and prevent them.

The Schizophrenias – well-known, less-known and unknown

Well-known
1. Dementia paralytica
2. Pellagra
3. Porphyria
4. Hypothyroidism
5. Drug intoxications
6. Homocysteinuria
7. Folic acid/B_{12} deficiency
8. Sleep deprivation
9. Heavy metal toxicity

   Less well-known
   1. Hypoglycaemia
   2. Psychomotor epilepsy
   3. Cerebral allergy
   4. Wheat-gluten sensitivity
   5. Histapenia – copper excess
   6. Histadelia
   7. Pyroluria
   8. Wilson's disease
   9. Chronic candida infection
   10. Huntington's chorea

      Almost unknown
      1. Prostaglandins
      2. Dopamine excess
      3. Endorphins
      4. Serine excess
      5. Prolactin excess
      6. Dialysis therapy
      7. Serotonin imbalance
      8. Leucine, histidine imbalance
      9. Interferon, amantadine,
         Anti-viral drugs, any drug toxicity
      10. Platelets deficient in MHO

3

Anxiety and Phobias – The Copper Connection

The problem patients who come to the Brain Bio Center for help routinely have a battery of tests, including one for histamine. Histamine is an important brain chemical and is involved in all sorts of reactions, including those to pain and allergies, causing tears to flow, excessive mucus, saliva and other bodily secretions. On careful study of the data from thousands of schizophrenic patients, we found that 50 per cent have a low blood level of histamine which rises to normal levels as they improve. This is called histapenia.

What causes low histamine?
The histapenic patient is not only low in histamine but also has tissues that are loaded with copper. Thus, both histamine depletion and copper excess may produce behavioural abnormalities. Instead of blaming the family, or the 'schizophrenic mother' who is accused of loving her offspring too much or too little, the finding of high copper in a patient's blood shifts the blame to the environment – usually to the copperized drinking water resulting from the use of copper in water pipes.

Mothers and children drink the same water so they can all be poisoned by the environment. Most fathers are away from home during the day so their copper burden and copper-induced 'schizophrenia' may be less. The concept grows that some metals now called trace elements or micronutrients, such as zinc and manganese, may be deficient, or copper may be in excess, in some types of 'schizophrenias'.

The low-histamine or histapenic person also has some distinctive characteristics, as shown below. These are most pronounced in histapenic schizophrenics, but they exist in a diminished form in a large proportion of the general population.

Are you histapenic?

Do you have any of these characteristics?

1. Canker sores
2. Difficult orgasm with sex
3. No headaches or allergies
4. Heavy growth of body hair
5. Excess fat in lower extremities
6. Many dental fillings
7. Ideas of grandeur
8. Undue suspicion of people
9. The feeling that someone controls your mind
10. Seeing or hearing things abnormally
11. The ability to stand pain well
12. Ringing in the ears

If so you will benefit from:

1. Niacin, 100mg, a.m. and p.m. (causes a blushing sensation)
2. Niacinamide, 250-500mg, a.m. and p.m.
3. Folic acid, 1,000mcg each a.m.
4. B_{12} injection, weekly or daily supplementation
5. L-Tryptophan, 1,000mg at bedtime
6. Zinc and manganese daily
7. High-protein diet

While the patient who is high in histamine may have depression, obsession and suicide, disperception and thought disorder, histapenic patients have all the classic symptoms of 'schizophrenia', including anxiety, paranoia and hallucinations.

Trace elements - the missing link

Schizophrenics may have low levels of zinc and manganese and high levels of copper, iron, mercury or lead. The last two are, of course, poisons, but the poisoning may produce symptoms which mimic those of 'schizophrenia'. This has been well documented for mercury and lead. For the 'porphyric' schizophrenic, such as King George III, the suggestion of a need for extra dietary zinc goes back to 1929, when Derrien and Benoit found a high level of zinc in the urine of patients with excessive amounts of the body chemical porphyrin. They suggested that zinc deficiency might be the cause of the abnormal psychiatric symptoms. The excess loss of zinc by the chelating action of uroporphyrin has been confirmed by other researchers (Watson and Schwartz in 1941, Nesbitt in 1944, and Peters in 1961). In 1965, two Japanese researchers (Kimura and Kumura) found that brain autopsy specimens from schizophrenics contained approximately half the zinc found in the brains of patients dying of other causes.

Other than copper studies, very few studies of trace metals appear in the literature on schizophrenia, even though the use of trace metals as a possible treatment of the disease began in 1929. At that time Dr English of Brookville, Ontario, reported on the use of manganese injections in 181 schizophrenic patients and found that about half of them improved. As with drug therapy (chlorpromazine and reserpine), Dr English reported a gain in weight in those patients who responded to manganese therapy (intravenous manganese produced a cutaneous flush like that of niacin!). Dr English got the idea of the use of manganese from Dr Reiter of Denmark who, in 1927, found that twenty-three out of thirty patients improved with manganese. Sadly, these studies were later repeated wrongly by R. Hoskins of the Worcester Foundation in 1934. Instead of using manganese chloride intravenously he used, for the most part, suspended manganese dioxide given intramuscularly. In the first instance, the intravenous route was unnecessary with water soluble and orally absorbed manganese chloride. In the second instance, manganese dioxide is a non-absorbable form, deposited intramuscularly, where it probably stayed for a very long time. Not surprisingly, Hoskins found no improvement in the small group of schizophrenics injected with manganese dioxide and manganese was promptly forgotten about for the next twenty years. We find that supplementing manganese and zinc helps speed up the excretion of excess copper.

The copper controversy

One of the earliest studies implicating high copper in schizophrenia was carried out in 1941 by Dr Heilmeyer and colleagues. They reported findings of elevated serum copper levels in twenty-three out of thirty-seven schizophrenics. In subsequent studies the same authors found similar serum copper elevation in some manic depressives and epileptics, and also in some cases of alcohol intoxication, infectious disease and cancer. Modern analytic techniques have since confirmed the frequent prevalence of high-copper individuals suffering from these disorders.

These original findings did stimulate some interest in copper research in schizophrenia and the details of high copper were essentially verified by several workers in the subsequent years (Brenner, 1949; Jantz, 1950; and Bischoff, 1952). Brenner made an extensive study of the serum copper levels in childhood 'schizophrenia' under different physiological and pathological conditions. In children with definite schizophrenic symptoms, he found extremely high serum copper levels, in contrast to the findings for children with mental retardation and other brain disorders. Brenner also found that more than a third of adult schizophrenics had high copper levels, which were not detectable during periods of spontaneous remission. But not all researchers have had such positive results (Munch-Peterson 1950).

A very careful and well-controlled study on copper metabolism in 122 schizophrenics was performed by Ozek (1957). No less than two-thirds of patients had high copper levels, especially among those described as having an 'acute' condition. (No difference in the red blood cell levels of copper or ceruloplasmin levels was detected. Ceruloplasmin is the copper containing serum protein which contains the enzyme, serum oxidase.)

Differences in the clinical symptoms and responses of low and high blood histamine patients

	Histapenia (50 per cent)	Histadelia (20 per cent)
Psychiatric symptoms		
Suicidal depression	1+	4+
'Blank mind'	1+	4+
Thought disorder	4+	2+
Paranoia	3+	1+
Hallucinations	4+	1+
Obsessions	1+	4+
Phobias	1+	4+
Metabolic differences		
Serum copper	above 100	below 100
Serum zinc	below 100	100
Basophil count per cu mm	below 30	above 50
Headaches	1+	4+
Fat distribution	stalagmitic	normal
Speed to orgasm	slow	fast
Reaction to pain	1+	4+
Dental caries	4+	1+
Salivary flow	1+	4+
Head colds (symptoms)	none	normal
Skin pigmentation	fair	normal
Allergies	rare	common
EEG over-arousal	4+	4+
Familial disorder	1+	3+
Age at onset	any	adult

Responses to therapy

Antipsychotic drug treatment	3+	1+
Niacin/vitamin C	3+	1+
Folic acid, 2.5 mg/day	3+ (sometimes dramatic!)	worsens
High-protein diet	yes	no
ECT/insulin	3+	1+
Methadone and some anti-histamines	0	3+
Zinc and manganese therapy	2+	3+
Phenytion therapy (Dilantin)	worsens	benefits

Note: 4+ means 'extremely common'
        1+ means 'uncommon'

In 1957, Dr Ackerfeldt reported elevated levels of the copper-based enzyme, serum oxidase, in adult schizophrenics. He was the first to make this observation. This was then confirmed in a study of 250 schizophrenics (Abood, 1957) which also found abnormally high ceruloplasmin and oxidase levels. However, these researchers considered dietary factors, liver damage and chronic infections as possible contributory factors. Meanwhile, preliminary experiments were indicating that excitement tends to elevate ceruloplasmin. Normal people receiving a synthetic hallucinatory drug demonstrated the same elevated ceruloplasmin level as psychotic schizophrenics. Other workers (Horwitt et al, 1957: Frank and Wurtman, 1958: Scheinberg et al, 1957) were unable to find significant differences in ceruloplasmin oxidase activity in schizophrenic children and adults as compared with controls.

In 1962, Dr Michael Briggs of Wellington, New Zealand theorized that many cases of 'schizophrenia' were really cases of chronic copper poisoning. This theory was based on the higher copper levels found in many schizophrenics which explained altered body chemistry.

In the next decade, research into copper accelerated, and more and more evidence accumulated to confirm the copper connection.

But not all studies were positive. What was the missing factor? Out of twenty groups of scientists who have studied copper levels in schizophrenics, fifteen considered 'schizophrenia' as a homogeneous clinical entity. Only four groups of scientists allowed for the possibility that 'simplistic schizophrenia' is a diagnosis made out of reluctant desperation. We had found that a sub-group of about 50 per cent of our diagnosed 'schizophrenic' patients were high in copper. These patients often experienced paranoia and hallucinations. With nutritional therapy designed to reduce the copper burden of the body, the paranoia and hallucinations improved. The antidote was extra zinc, or zinc and manganese. Unlike many researchers, we did not study the hodgepodge 'simplistic schizophrenia' but studied each patient in depth over a period of months and years with a blood sample taken for copper, zinc, manganese and many other biochemical markers at each visit. Some of our patients have been studied for twenty years.

Vitamin B₃ combats copper

The histapenic patient has many similarities to pellagra patients. Pellagra, caused by B₃ deficiency, was prevalent in the Southern States of America in the 1940's. Doctors Findlay and Venter found that pellagra sufferers were also high in copper. In India in 1974, Doctor Krishnamachavi studied copper in pellagra patients and found an abnormally high level which dropped with niacin (B₃) treatment. These findings, backed up by the fact that hair copper and urinary excretion of copper are also high in this vitamin deficient state, indicated that B₃ deficiency causes copper levels to rise, making B₃ another potential antidote to copper.

Vitamin C deficiency raises copper levels

Dr Yvonne Hitier of France studied copper levels in guinea pigs on a diet deficient in vitamin C. As the animals became C-deficient, the copper levels in the blood serum rose steadily until a level 2.5 times higher than normal was reached at death. This is a vicious circle in that high copper levels are known to destroy vitamin C. This may, in part, explain why the early treatment of mental illness with large doses of vitamins B_3 and C often helped patients. Two tentative conclusions might be drawn:

1. High copper may produce a mental illness similar to that of B_3-deficiency pellagra.

2. The combined deficiency of both vitamins B_3 and C may synergistically raise copper levels.

The birth control pill raises copper

It is a well-established fact that ceruloplasmin, the copper-containing protein, is produced faster in the presence of the female hormone, oestrogen, and women taking contraceptive pills uniformly exhibit raised copper levels. It is also interesting to note that any biological state which elevates the serum copper is apt to increase the need of vitamin C. So both mental illness, late pregnancy and particularly the use of the contraceptive pill produce states of elevated copper levels, which in turn may aggravate depression and disperception in schizophrenic patients on the pill. Animals given oestrogen show a marked reduction in blood levels of vitamin C. For women, vitamin C levels are highest at ovulation and lowest during menstruation, so cyclical problems may again be tied in with copper and vitamin C.

In summary, high levels of copper can cause mental illness, often characterized by extreme fears, paranoia and hallucinations. The copper may be the result of drinking water passing through copper pipes, copper pots and pans, the contraceptive pill and even copper IUDs. Or it can be the result of vitamin C or B_3 deficiency. Either way, copper lowers histamine and as histamine levels return to normal so does the high-copper, low-histamine individual. The next chapter looks at the other side of the coin – high histamine.

4

High Histamine Can Cause Depression

Histamine isn't only a problem if it's low. It's also a problem if it's high. Unlike low histamine, high histamine, called histadelia, is mostly an inherited trait. Since histamine speeds up metabolism, providing more heat, and since vitamin C is an anti-histamine, we think that when people lose the ability to make vitamin C, a fate they share only with guinea pigs, flying bats and other primates, this puts them at an advantage in colder climates during and after the Ice Age.

But histamine also causes allergic reactions, increased production of mucus and saliva, a tendency to hyperactivity, compulsive behaviour and depression. Some of these traits can be an advantage, but when histamine levels are not controlled, they can lead to chronic depression and even suicide. Marilyn Monroe, Judy Garland and Shane McNeill, son of Eugene McNeill, are three examples of likely histadelics who died a suicidal death.

Are you histadelic?

Do you:

1. Sneeze in bright sunlight?
2. Feel you were shy and over-sensitive as a teenager?
3. Cry, salivate and feel nauseous easily?
4. Hear your pulse in your head on the pillow at night?
5. Get referred itches when you scratch your leg?
6. Have frequent back aches, stomach aches, muscle cramps?
7. Have easy orgasm with sex?

8. Have regular headaches and seasonal allergies?
9. Have inner tension and occasional depression?
10. Have abnormal fears, compulsions, rituals?
11. Think you are a light sleeper?
12. Burn up foods rapidly?
13. Think frequently of suicide?
14. Tolerate a lot of alcohol and other 'downers'?
15. Have little body hair and a lean build?
16. Have large ears and long fingers and toes?
17. Belong to an all-boy family?

If so you will respond to:

1. A low-protein, high-complex carbohydrate diet
2. Calcium (as gluconate), 500mg, a.m. and p.m.
3. Methionine, 500mg, a.m. and p.m.
   and (if seriously depressed) you may need:
4. Judicious use of anti-convulsant drugs

But you should avoid folic acid and multivitamins which contain folic acid because these can raise histamine levels.

The histadelic patient comprises about 20 per cent of the schizophrenics. This estimate is based on the many patients who were treated over the twenty-one year period from 1966 to 1987 at the Brain Bio Center. The histadelic person is often the problem patient at psychiatric clinics and hospitals.

Our first contact with histadelia occured in a biochemical and psychiatric study of out-patient schizophrenics. Two out of nine chronic patients on whom we had extensive data and repeated visits showed significant positive correlations between blood histamine and the Experimental World Inventory (EWI), a psychological measure of stability. In other words, both the highly-elevated EWI score and the blood histamine decreased as the patient got better.

A familial disorder
Histadelia usually runs in families, with the onset at around 20

years of age. The easily elicited history of suicide, depression and allergies among near and distant relatives is a strong indication of possible histadelia. This disorder has probably been termed familial psychotic depression in the past. The undiagnosed histadelic patient is treated as a schizophrenic but the patient does not respond to any of the usual drug therapies, electro-shock or insulin coma therapy. We have now treated over 1,000 of these patients and our experience provides many important signs that help in making early diagnosis. Early diagnosis is important since suicide is a constant threat for the histadelic.

Histadelics are compulsive people
Disperceptions, obsessions, compulsions, thought disorder, blank mind, abnormal fears, constant suicidal depression, easy crying and confusion may all occur. The symptom of blank mind is elicited by asking if the patient can visualize the face of her mother or visualize why, on a motorway, she might be directed to turn left though she actually wants to turn right on to a new motorway (clover leaf turn). She often cannot visualize these things.

These people are fast oxidizers and may have drug, alcohol and sugar addiction. Histamine furthers rapid oxidation of foodstuffs so the histadelic patient may be the thin individual with the hollow leg: 'I can eat or drink anything without gaining weight.'

Metabolic symptoms
Because of the high histamine level the histadelic can cry at the slightest provocation. Histamine produces a good flow of saliva so the teeth are frequently free of cavities. The metabolic rate is high so the patient has minimal fat – an attractive body figure is the result. Since Marilyn Monroe was probably histadelic we can, at this late date, understand better her remark to news photographers, 'You always take pictures of my body but my most perfect feature is my teeth – I have no cavities.' With good salivary flow teeth are well bathed in saliva and the histadelic may have the habit of wiping saliva from the corners of the mouth with thumb and index finger. Like a drug addict, he may be hooked on excess sugar in

coffee or tea. A history of allergies or periodic headache and sensitivity to pain is also common. When blood is taken or an injection of B_{12} is given, the patient may cry out or squirm because he has a very low pain threshold. Patients will not have excessive body or extremity hair. In men the beard is usually light. The natural hair colour is usually brunette or black. The histadelic usually has an easy and well sustained orgasm and therefore the label of nymphomania may occasionally be applied. We have also seen some depressed children with high blood histamine but these children frequently have lead poisoning which also raises blood histamine. Histadelic patients have the most severe insomnia of any subdivision of the 'schizophrenias'. Doses of five 100mg pentobarbital tablets are often needed at bedtime, along with chlorpromazine, to get a good night's sleep. One such patient living alone swallowed and slept through a dose of twenty-seven pentobarbital capsules! Ordinarily, we medics worry about ten being swallowed at a single dose.

Drugs don't help

These overtreated and mistreated patients have frequently made the rounds of the best psychiatric hospitals where large doses of chlorpromazine or fluphenazine are often ineffective. Electro-shock does little and insulin coma therapy is useless. The patient on 10mg fluphenazine may seem like a wooden statue because of the drug-induced muscle effects – and the psychiatrist may now say catatonia has set in! This catatonia, of course, responds to a decrease in the fluphenazine dosage or the daily use of Cogentin – an antidote to the muscle contractions. The anti-depressant drugs such as amitriptyline or MAO inhibitors (Parstelin or Nardil) are ineffective. Lithium in a low dose of 600-900mg per day is somewhat effective; larger doses are not more effective. L-tryptophan in the usual dose of 1g at bedtime may produce a prolonged two to three hour blushing sensation and cardiovascular reaction, apparently because of the histadelic's rapid conversion of tryptophan to the brain chemical, serotonin.

Vitamins C and B$_3$ don't help either

Nor do these people respond to the classical meganutrient (B$_3$, vitamin C) therapy first used by Drs Hoffer and Osmond. If the B vitamin, folic acid, is given, the patient definitely gets worse. B$_{12}$ injection is tolerated, however, and may moderate depression.

What does work is calcium supplementation, which releases some of the body's stores of histamine, and the natural amino acid methionine, which helps to detoxify histamine by methylation – the usual mode of detoxification of histamine in the human body. Phenytoin, the anti-epilepsy drug (trade marked Dilantin in the USA) is also an anti-folic acid drug. Phenytoin in a dose of 100mg, a.m. and p.m., will usually provide some relief for the severely depressed or compulsive patient. However, the methionine plus calcium combined with zinc and manganese is often sufficient so we can sometimes omit the use of phenytoin. The same regime of zinc, manganese, calcium, methionine (and phenytoin) provides successful treatment in many severely allergic patients who are not depressed. The most effective diet may be one that is low in protein with adequate vegetables and fruit.

Testing for histamine

Few laboratories can actually test histamine levels in the blood (see Useful Addresses on page 123) which is the best way of determining your histamine status, but most of the histamine in the body resides in a type of white blood cell called a basophil. This is easily measured by any routine blood-testing laboratory and a high basophil count is highly predictive of histadelia. As the histadelic is often allergic, he may have a high level of IgE, a blood protein involved in inhalant allergic reactions. Alternatively, he may have responded to allergy skin tests.

As with all chronic depressives, the prognosis in histadelia must be cautiously guarded. Patients may stop their nutritional programme, become suicidal, and the grim reaper may win. In general, if the patient stays with the nutritional programme, the depressions and compulsions are kept in check. For example, we started treating one young man for histadelia ten years ago. He had been in mental hospitals from the age of 17 until he was 26. However, he has not been hospitalized since our treatment commenced and is now a productive citizen. While depression is often lifted early on, compulsions with abnormal fears are the most difficult to treat and are also the last symptom to go.

Drug addicts are histadelic

Having tested twelve hard-core drug addicts and found them all to be high in histamine, we voice the strong opinion that more can be done to correct biochemical imbalance in the drug addict. We know that heroin and methadone are both strong histamine releasing agents. The histadelic person is depressed, compulsive and has abnormal thinking. Therefore heroine, methadone, uppers, downers, alcohol and sugar are often craved to compensate for these feelings. The compulsive day-in-day-out drinker of alcohol is usually found to be histadelic. Moderation must be taught tactfully to these individuals as they slowly but surely improve on the nutrition.

The threat of suicide

The greatest problem in the severely depressed histadelic is the constant threat of suicide. An understanding relative or spouse living with the patient is the best safeguard. Character disorder, as in the drug addict, is always a problem and the remembrance of how high and powerful the patient felt on drugs is a problem. We can never meet this degree of mental over-alertness with good nutrition. We can make the patient feel normal but not hypomanic. For some of these compulsive patients normality is just not enough.

5

B₆ and Zinc – The Missing Link

Perhaps the most significant discovery in the nutritional treatment of mental illness is that many depressed and mentally ill people are deficient in vitamin B_6 and zinc. But this deficiency is no ordinary deficiency that is simply corrected by eating more foods that are rich in zinc and B_6. It is connected with the abnormal production of a group of chemicals called 'pyrroles'. A patient with a high level of pyrroles in the urine needs more B_6 and zinc, since these pyrroles rob the body of these essential nutrients. About 30 per cent of schizophrenics have 'pyroluria', and 11 per cent of 'normals' have it as well.

Are you pyroluric?

Do you have disperceptions and some of the following?

1. Intolerance to some protein foods, alcohol or drugs.
2. Definite breath and body odour.
3. Morning nausea and constipation.
4. Difficulty remembering your dreams.
5. Crowded upper front teeth.
6. White spots on your finger nails.
7. Pale skin which doesn't tolerate sunlight.
8. Frequent upper abdominal pain.
9. Frequent head colds and infections.
10. Stretch marks in the skin.
11. Irregular menstrual cycle or impotency.
12. Any of the above when stressed.

13. You belong to an all-girl family with look-alike sisters.

If so you will benefit from:

1. Vitamin B_6 each a.m. – enough for nightly dream recall (do not exceed 2,000mg!).
2. Zinc (as the gluconate), 30mg, a.m. and p.m.
3. Manganese (as the gluconate), 10mg, a.m. and p.m.

Closely ranked in creativity to the compulsive productivity of the histadelic patient is the 'pyroluric' patient. Many great people in history have shown the signs of pyroluria. Among these are the poet, Emily Dickinson, and the scientific philosopher and discoverer, Charles Darwin. Their life stories reflect many of the character traits associated with this condition.

Pyroluria – the reason for adult withdrawal and seclusion?
Reflections on the meaning of life and death were the two major influences in the life works of both Emily Dickinson and Charles Darwin. Their literary and scientific contributions have been praised for over a century, but only recently has science begun to look into their secluded lives and gather the pertinent data that suggests that Emily Dickinson and Charles Darwin may have suffered biochemical abnormalities which produced the physical and psychiatric symptoms of pyroluria.

They both possessed great originality and drive. Because of this creativity they feared and avoided any outside stress that might upset their delicate balance of emotion and ideas. Any change in routine or involvement with people outside the family group provoked stress which could manifest itself as a tremor, palpitations, insomnia and (for Darwin) nausea and vomiting as well. As Darwin and Dickinson approached the age of 30 they purposely chose voluntary exile. Emily was succinctly subjective when she wrote, 'The soul selects her own society then shuts the door'.

An amalgam of pyroluric symptoms manifested themselves during the course of their isolated lives. They shared bouts of depression, blinding headaches, nervous exhaustion, a change of handwriting and a familial dependence. Darwin endured, usually without complaint, a crippling fatigue and loss of appetite and underwent such extreme depression that it pained him to look at a printed page. Emily became hypersensitive to normal daylight and suffered such extreme eye pains that she, too, could not read.

Medical and psychological authorities have claimed emotional, psychological or simple physical reasons for the reclusiveness of Dickinson and Darwin. For them, seclusion may have been a means by which they could combat the distressing symptoms of pyroluria. A cloistered life provided them with regulated daily routine and diet, adequate rest and, most important, the avoidance of stressful situations and experiences that enabled them to continue their brilliant studies and productive writing. Emily Dickinson gave her personal explanation when she wrote 'Insanity for the sane seems so unreasonable'.

Because of her strict seclusion, medical data on Emily Dickinson is scant. We do know that Emily only wore white dresses. Both Dickinson and Darwin worshipped their protective fathers, and were severely grieved by their fathers' deaths. As they slipped deeper into seclusion, their handwriting changed and became less legible. When young, both Dickinson and Darwin enjoyed the company of friends and going to parties. However, as they grew older they became retiring and avoided even the closest friends, except through correspondence. Certainly pyroluria occurs in our most original psychiatric patients and therefore deserves first consideration as an explanation when the illnesses of Emily Dickinson and Charles Darwin are reviewed.

How pyroluria was discovered

The first time urinary excretion of pyrroles was connected with psychosis was in 1958, when a Canadian doctor, Dr Payza, noted a new substance in the urine of several patients undergoing experimental LSD model psychosis. The abnormal chemical found in the urine of these patients was later found in the urine of many psychiatric patients who had never taken LSD or any other drug. In 1961, Drs Abram Hoffer and Mahon found the 'mauve factor' in twenty-seven out of thirty-nine schizophrenic patients. (The extracted urine made a lavender colour when reacted with Ehrlich's Reagent.) One-third of the psychiatric patients with diagnosis other than 'schizophrenia' also had the mauve factor in their urine. In 1963, Drs Hoffer and Osmond coined the word 'malvaria' to designate mauve positive patients. O'Reilly and Hughes (1965), studying normals and psychiatric patients, found the mauve factor in 11 per cent normals, 24 per cent of disturbed children, 42 per cent of psychiatric patients and 52 per cent of schizophrenics. But the scientist who really solved the mauve factor enigma was Donald Irvine of Saskatoon in Canada. He found the exact structure of the mauve factor to be the chemical, kryptopyrrole, which was then confirmed by Dr Arthur Sohler of the Brain Bio Center. We suggested that kryptopyrrole would produce a severe B_6 deficiency (since pyrroles bind to aldehydes, and pyridoxal (B_6) is an aldehyde). This was confirmed and we further found that the complex of pyridoxal with kryptopyrrole took excess zinc out of the body.

With this knowledge, effective therapy was at hand and the mauve factor patients got well when treated with both vitamin B_6 and zinc. With this discovery the term 'pyroluria' was coined. Since 1971 we have seen over 1,000 pyroluric patients and most of them have responded well to B_6 and zinc therapy.

Pyroluria equals a real life family tragedy

Do you remember the French film *Story of a Cheat*, starring Sacha Guitry, which opened with eleven coffins being carted slowly down the tree-edged road? The cheat (played by a 10-year-old boy) walked behind the coffins. He had been naughty so had been sent to bed without any supper the night before. Supper had consisted of mushrooms gathered in the woods but the mushrooms were poisonous and the entire family died, hence the parade of coffins. Because he had been bad he, the cheat, had lived. A dramatic opener indeed but fortunately just a story.

Pyroluria, on the other hand, often produces a real family tragedy. Consider the story of one of our patients.

A pyroluric doctor married a pyroluric nurse. The outcome of the marriage was four children and three miscarriages. One of the miscarriages was a boy. The sex of the other two was never determined. Four daughters lived, but by the age of 20, three of them had been labelled schizophrenic. With these labels we have the possibility of three walking corpses out of a family of four children. When there is pyroluria in the family, the boys are miscarried or stillborn, or have birth defects, while the daughters live normally until stressed at the age of 15–20 years. With stress, the daughters will have psychiatric difficulties and this usually occurs in the last years of school or the first years of college. The stress may cause depression (suicide) or disperceptions and hallucinations.

The family provides the clues to pyroluria

In Wilson's disease where the tissue level of copper is high, the neurologist may frequently make a diagnosis by doing tests on a brother or sister. In such a familial disease a low copper protein level in one child makes all other children suspect. Only the prepared mind can make such a diagnosis, or as the old doctor said, 'you can't diagnose it unless you think of it'. The same is true with pyroluria.

In pyroluria, suicide of one member of a family may be the dramatic event which should alert the doctor to the possibility of pyroluria in other sisters or brothers. Unless this diagnosis is considered, all the living relatives may be inadequately treated for their easily treatable mental disorder. If untreated, pyroluria may result in another family tragedy.

Our most tragic double loss was a pyroluric–histadelic family from a distant city. This was in the 1960s, before we knew how to treat pyroluria. The patient was under the careful care of the psychiatrist who referred him for diagnosis. We found a high kryptopyrrole in his urine and a very high blood level of histamine. Shortly after that he shot himself dead. His younger brother, who was in the army, was informed of the tragic death and went insane. The army treated this stress-induced insanity with large doses of chlorpromazine. The younger brother developed bone marrow suppression and died of aplastic anaemia. Two family deaths within one year.

Patients got well for no discernible reason

During 1967 and 1971, when we were vigorously applying vitamins to patients, we found that some young patients improved rapidly although they were neither high nor low in blood histamine. We were also measuring pyrroles in their urine and finally came to the conclusion that these young patients improved as the pyrrole levels decreased and the dose of vitamin B_6 was increased. The patients were on zinc supplements since we knew that histamine was stored with zinc in the terminal buds of the nerve cells. Later in 1971 a dramatic case provided the necessary data to link pyroluria with zinc and B_6 deficiency. Consider Sara's story.

Since she was 11, Sara's life had been a nightmare of mental and bodily suffering. Her history included chronic insomnia, episodic loss of reality, attempted suicide by hanging, amnesia, partial seizures, nausea, vomiting and loss of periods. Her knees were so painful (X-rays showed poor cartilages) and her mind so disperceptive that she walked slowly with her feet wide apart like a peasant following a hand plough drawn by tired oxen. Her brain wave and standard blood tests were within normal limits. Groups of psychiatrists, both juvenile and adult specialists at three different hospitals gave the dubious waste-basket labels of 'schizophrenia', 'paranoid schizophrenia' and 'schizophrenia with convulsive disorder'. At times her left side went into spasms with foot clawed and fist doubled up. Both arm and leg had a wild flaying motion. Restraints were needed at these times. Psychotherapy was ineffective and most tranquillizers accentuated the muscle symptoms. Urinary kryptopyrrole was at times as high as 1,000mcg%, the normal range being less than 15. She was diagnosed as B_6 and zinc deficient and treatment was started.

Sara responds to zinc and B₆

We learned many facts about pyroluria as we got Sara well over a period of three months:

1. Her knees needed adequate zinc and manganese to develop normal cartilage and tendons.

2. Her brain needed adequate B_6 to prevent the abnormal messages which cause convulsive seizures.

3. Her brain was alive with abnormal cross-talk between neurones which gave the final behaviour of depression, amnesia and disperceptions.

4. Her bone marrow produced inadequate synthesis of haemoglobin resulting in anaemia and pyrroles in her urine.

5. Her endocrine glands required adequate zinc and B_6 to establish a normal menstrual cycle.

6. Her spleen and liver (like other patients with rupture of red cells) became engorged periodically with red cell debris to produce a severe upper abdominal pain. Sara walked completely bent over when she had this pain.

7. Sara (like the B_6 pregnant woman) had nausea each morning when she did not get her morning dose of vitamin B_6.

8. Sara (like a class of patients labelled schizophrenic) had a fruity odour to her breath and sweat.

9. Sara reacted adversely to tranquillizers and barbiturates because her tissue enzymes were B_6 deficient and could not detoxify the drugs.

10. Finally, observation of Sara's symptoms and biochemistry allowed the explanation of an easily treatable type of schizophrenia in spite of three such hospital rubber-stamped labels. She has had no recurrence of her grave illness and has now finished college and works in New York City. She takes

zinc and B_6 daily. When under stress of any kind, she increases her intake of vitamin B_6.

Mark Vonnegut (the son of Kurt Vonnegut) wrote *Eden Express* after recovery from pyroluria. Mark was stricken with insomnia which led to 'crazies' while in college. His book must be read to learn the difficulties that the patient encounters in mental hospitals. Mark had severe pyroluria when tested at the Brain Bio Center in February 1973. He showed the usual rapid improvement when given daily zinc and enough B_6 to produce dream recall. The big event of 1973 was our discovery that B_6-deficient patients had no dream recall. With adequate B_6 they remember the last dream of the night. With too much B_6, a patient may awaken every two hours during the night with vivid dreams – and remember up to four dreams in the morning.

Dream recall is a normal event in a healthy individual
Knowing that we are concerned with nutrition and chemistry, some patients have a perplexed look when we ask about dream recall. Some say they have not dreamed since childhood and therefore believe that only children dream enough to be able to tell their dreams at the breakfast table. Not so! Many original adults will use their dreams to re-vitalize their minds and their daily productivity. For instance, Dave Brubeck, the musician, told us that in his younger days he got ideas for musical composition from dreams. For a period the dreams vanished but now with adequate daily B_6 intake, he has vivid dreams which again help his musical composition and complex arrangements.

When patients ask us why we want them to have better dream recall, I simply state, 'Dream recall is normal. We want you to be normal.' One pyroluric patient called excitedly to relate that the first new dream he had was about the terrible time he had had in the mental hospital (a real id catharsis). He asked if I had planned that for him. Because of my usual busy day I said 'Yes' and went on to the next dreamless patient.

Another 13-year old young lady who had only had nightmares

in the last two years now found that she had pleasant dreams. Her only comment was that 'Some of my dreams are awfully sexy.' I responded by saying pragmatically that at least she wouldn't get pregnant from dreams. She replied, 'Oh! I wouldn't go that far even in my dreams!'

Yet another 17-year-old patient had her nightmares changed to pleasant dreams. Her psychoanalyst protested that nightmares were useful for the elimination of inner aggression and that the change to pleasant dreams was a step backwards! I sided with the patient who liked the pleasant dreams. Others apply our findings to diagnose and help the pyroluric. At least twenty clinics around the USA and a few in Europe do pyrrole testing of the urine and carry out zinc and B$_6$ treatment with pyroluric patients. A few orthodox clinics are having success, as reported in the medical journals.

'Zinc Deficiency Presenting as Schizophrenia' is the title of an article published by Drs Stanton, Donald and Green, in *Current Psychiatric Digest*, in December 1976. These doctors work at the Psychiatric Institute of Columbia, South Carolina and point out the need to study zinc and copper relationships in psychotic patients.

Their zinc-deficient psychiatric patient was an 18-year-old teenager from Carolina, off to college as a music major in California. Under social stress at college he became agitated and when admitted to a California medical centre was found to be disorientated as to time and place and bothered by constant visual and auditory hallucinations. He did not respond to medication (Prolixon and Haldol). He returned to South Carolina and was committed into a mental hospital for further study and treatment. The only laboratory abnormality among the routine tests was elevation of the liver enzymes SGOT, SGPT, and LDH, all of which rise with B$_6$ deficiency. Other drugs were tried without success. He had episodes of elevated blood pressure, 150/120 – a sign of copper excess. He was delusional, hallucinating, self-destructive and when questioned he slowly repeated the words of the examining doctor. A series of fifteen electro-convulsive shock treatments (ECT) were given with some temporary improvement but within ten days of the ECT the patient was back to the original psychotic baseline and attempted to jump through a window.

'Tug of war'

Figure 4. The trace elements have a 'tug of war' with the heavy metals in the body.

Zinc found to be low and copper high

When all else failed, trace metal levels were run on his blood serum. The zinc was 65mcg % (our normal being 100–120) and copper was 185 (our normal being 100mcg % for males). In the words of the authors: 'Because all other treatment had proven ineffective it was decided to treat the patient as if he were pyroluric and attempt to replace the zinc and B_6.'

On 160mg zinc sulphate per day and 1,000mg B_6 twice a day, the patient became quiet in two days. He was more alert and was able to leave his locked room and join other patients in the ward. His muscle rigidity and tremor lessened. Progress was steady and within one month the patient was emotionally normal, making plans for the future and fully cogniscient of the world about him. His tested degree of insanity (In-patient Behaviour Scale) went from a high of 71 to a normal of 10 at discharge. Follow-up at one year found him back at college and doing well, his zinc level was still low (75mcg %) but his copper level was normal at 90mcg %. The patient co-operates fully and continues to take his daily dose of zinc and B$_6$.

The doctors conclude: 'We do believe that there exists a group of patients who have a zinc deficiency which, complicated by emotional stress, may present a schizophrenic picture. Because of the success and safety of the treatment, it would seem worthwhile to attempt to identify and treat such patients.' I can only say, in 1987, a fervent 'Amen! Let's do it'.

Other symptoms and signs of pyroluria

Sara had at least ten of the clinical features which may characterize pyroluria. With almost ten years of experience we can easily add as many more signs and symptoms. In so doing we can clarify more exactly the nature of pyroluria.

It is a stress-induced disorder, the symptoms of which will usually diminish when the degree of stress is lessened. Pyroluria can be a life-long disorder with miscarriage of male children (all-girl families), stillbirths, slow learning, mental retardation, infantile autism, delayed puberty, amnesia, 'schizophrenia', teenage depression or delinquency, allergic symptoms, and even cancer in the zenith of life. Most adults can predict and recognize stress in their life. For the child the parent must recognize stressful situations and, if possible, circumvent the stress. The stressful time for teenagers may be the first love affair, either homo or heterosexual (loss of virginity, homosexual panic), or the act of leaving home to live in a dormitory in college. Joining the armed forces is stressful and may precipitate illness if the patient is pyroluric.

Mental retardation from chronic B_6 and zinc deficiency

We have examined and treated children in the age range of 3–15 years who were labelled 'mentally retarded' or 'minimal brain disfunction' or 'learning disabled'. When the young patient has a high level of pyrroles in the urine, a low serum immunoglobulin A, and facial swelling with a history of frequent colds and middle ear infections, pyroluria should be suspected. The tissue swelling caused by zinc and B_6 deficiency prevents the adequate drainage of the auditory tubes from the middle ear to the throat. Immuno -globulin A (IgA) is present in all secretions of the body such as tears, mucus, saliva, breast milk, and gastric juices. When IgA is low there is poor resistance to infections and repeated infections may occur.

Pyrolurics do better on vegetarian diets

Vegetarians are usually thin and healthy, and fully one-third of the world's population are vegetarians because of religion and the high price of animal protein.

One patient from a southern city in the USA found that she could not eat any protein foods such as fish, chicken or red meat without developing unreality, dizziness and even hallucinations when she closed her eyes. Without fail, she was unduly suspicious of her companions whenever she ate meat – she had paranoia!

She thought she had an allergy to all proteins and she therefore came to us for food-allergy testing but on the initial tests we found her to be pyroluric with a high pyrrole level in her urine. We next found her to be both zinc and vitamin B_6 deficient, as are all pyroluric patients. Both zinc and B_6 are needed by the body to handle protein foods. With adequate vitamin B_6 plus zinc and manganese she found that she could tolerate proteins for the first time in many years. Furthermore, she started losing her fat and excess body fluids as a result of the new nutrients. She lost 15 pounds in weight in the short period of two months. Her dresses began to fit again.

The point to this case is that many disperceptive teenagers, when stressed, find that abnormal mental symptoms increase after a protein meal. They do feel better on an all-vegetarian diet and hence may not only become vegetarians but also join an Indian religious group which serves the vegetable meals. The abnormally disperceptive pyroluric patient is a sitting duck for far-out suggestions.

Autism responds to B$_6$ and zinc

We have known since 1970 that autistic children respond to zinc and B$_6$. Dr Allan Cott from New York was the first to confirm this finding. Dr Catherine Spears, a paediatric neurologist, reported that out of twenty autistic children she was treating, all responded to zinc and B$_6$. Dr Spears reports that parents, teachers and professionals have all rated the autistic children as improved in both behaviour and speech.

Dr Bernard Rimland of the Institute for Child Behavior Research in San Diego, California, listened to these reports and convinced his psychiatric colleagues that a controlled study of B$_6$ was feasible in autism. The study showed significant improvement in autism when B$_6$ was given. The sixteen patients also had magnesium and vitamin C in adequate supply. Rimland fought with the *American Journal of Psychiatry* to get it published and finally the article appeared in the April, 1978 issue (Vol. 135, page 474, 1978). *Science News* (113, May 13, 1978) summarizes the study wherein twelve out of sixteen autistic children improved on B$_6$ and regressed when dummy capsules were substituted for the vitamin.

Clues from skin, hair, teeth and nails

The pyroluric patient is often pale due to lack of skin pigment. This we have labelled a 'China Doll Appearance'. Zinc and B$_6$ are needed to produce pigment in both skin and hair. A pyroluric black patient will have the lightest skin of all the family. People who have never been able to have a skin tan (except albinos!) will tan normally on zinc and B$_6$. Local depigmentation (vitiligo) does not, unfortunately, respond to zinc therapy. The lack of hair on the head, eyelashes and eye brows can frequently be corrected with B_6 and zinc. The new hair will grow in the individual's natural colour, the same as before the deficiency occurred. We have seen prematurely grey hair return to black with zinc therapy. The loss of hair in the last month of pregnancy, and with the use of the pill, is due to high copper and low zinc levels produced by oestrogens.

The teeth in the upper jaw may be crowded unless the patient has had orthodontic treatment. This overcrowding shows when the patient smiles. The upper dental arch is narrow with overlapping incisors. The enamel of the teeth will be poor if the patient has been zinc-deficient during the period of tooth formation. Drs Curson and Losee find both copper and cadmium to be high in the enamel of decayed teeth compared with that in healthy teeth. Extra zinc is the antidote to high copper and cadmium levels in all tissues of the body. The gums may be red and retracted (pyorrhoea) where there is zinc deficiency. Good dental hygiene combined with zinc and B_6 will make the gums grow normally again.

The fingernails are white and spotted, opaquely white and tissue-paper thin in the pyroluric patient. The very thinness of the nails plus anxiety leads to active fingernail biting. The actual nails are no more solid than 'hang-nails' and everyone occasionally tears at hang-nails with the teeth. Small wonder nail biting occurs. As you know from that occasional blue spot under the nail, it takes six months to grow a new nail so the nails will be strong in six months with adequate intake of zinc and B_6. We confidently predict the cessation of nail biting in six months and our prediction seldom fails. Small white spots may resolve with zinc but large white spots require five to six months to grow out with the nail.

Skin infections respond to zinc and B_6

Acne, eczema and herpes (cold sores) may all respond to zinc and B_6 therapy. The avoidance of chocolate, nuts and thiamine, and supplementation with l-lysine also help get rid of herpes. Psoriasis is characterized by a high serum copper level so this may also respond to continued zinc and B$_6$ therapy. The effective treatment of severe skin disease may require as much as 60mg of zinc given two to three times per day, but this sort of dose should only be taken under supervision.

Summary

The careful study of people of all ages will find that about 10 per cent of a normal population have pyroluria which can cause symptoms when the patient is stressed. Among hospitalized schizophrenics the incidence of pyroluria will approach 30 per cent more.

Effective treatment is found in supplementing extra zinc and B$_6$. The adult dose of elemental zinc is 30mg (equivalent to 300mg zinc gluconate) taken a.m. and p.m. and enough vitamin B$_6$ should be given to produce normal dream recall. It is best not to take more than 500mg without proper supervision. The avoidance of stress is also helpful.

Pyroluria can occur at any age if familial, and can be the cause of mental retardation, minimal brain damage, epilepsy, hyperactivity, delinquency, amnesia, and one type of 'schizophrenia'.

6

Brain Allergies

The idea that food affects the mind is an alien concept to many people. But since the brain is perhaps the most delicate organ of the body, using sometimes as much as 30 per cent of all the energy we derive from food, this should be no surprise. Allergies to food can upset levels of hormones and other key chemicals in the brain, resulting in symptoms ranging from depression to schizophrenia.

The allergic patient whose mental symptoms are so severe as to merit the label of 'mentally ill' or even 'schizophrenic' has been known clinically for many years. As with many other biological types of the schizophrenias, the psychiatrists may be the last to learn and accept brain or cerebral allergy as a possible cause of some types of 'schizophrenia'.

The allergic child may suffer from the so-called 'allergic-tension-fatigue syndrome' described by Dr Frederic Speer in 1954, which results in irritability, hyperactivity and impaired concentration, thus adversely affecting school performance. Food dyes or additives may cause the symptoms. The most commonly implicated types of food are milk, wheat, egg, beef, corn, cane sugar and chocolate. A similar syndrome in adults has been called simply 'cerebral allergy'. The allergy often appears in a masked form, in which the individual actually feels better after ingesting a favourite food. However, in a variable number of hours a severe let-down occurs and the patient experiences symptoms which may be diffuse and non-specific and often include headache, depression, nasal stuffiness and sleepiness.

Allergies run in families

Allergy runs in families and so does cerebral allergy. The allergic diseases have many presenting symptoms and common names so that the infant who cannot tolerate cow's or goat's milk may be starting a life-long fight against allergies called colic, eczema or croup. Lack of breast-feeding may predispose the infant to allergies because the infant does not get the needed immune bodies from the mother. Colic may progress into coeliac disease wherein the food goes through the intestinal tract unchanged. If a sample of the intestinal wall is studied, it can be seen that the finger-like villi that absorb the food are missing and the intestinal wall is smooth and scarred. Asthma may occur and alternate with the other allergic diseases. Children eating food dyes or food naturally high in salicylates may develop hyperactivity.

Do you have cerebral allergies?

Do you have disperceptions and

1. A history of infantile colic
2. A history of infantile eczema
3. A history of coeliac disease (malabsorption)
4. A history of asthma, rashes or hay fever
5. Favourite daily foods
6. Excessive daily mood swings
7. Frequent rapid colds
8. Seasonal allergies
9. Relief of symptoms with fasting
10. Intolerance to foods such as wheat or milk.

If so, you will benefit from:

1. Methionine, 500mg, a.m. and p.m.
2. Calcium gluconate, 500mg, a.m. and p.m.
3. Zinc, 15mg, a.m. and p.m.
4. Manganese, 10mg (as gluconate), a.m. and p.m.
5. B_6 adequate for dream recall (no more than 2,000mg)
6. Vitamin C, 1,000–2,000mg, a.m. and p.m.

Food intolerance, lack of absorption of food and relief with fasting are three key pointers to the food-allergic patient. These patients usually have a low blood histamine, a fast pulse and food idiosyncrasies which may be expressed as strong likes and dislikes. Favourite foods are often the offending foods so the patients is like an addict, eating the offending food to obtain a psychiastric high.

What are the symptoms?

Extreme mood swings occurring within a single day may typify the cerebral allergic patient. These moods may be mania or deep depression and they correspond with the ingestion of foods. Many disperceptions, paranoia and abnormal thinking may be woven into a high or low mood. Fasting for twenty-four hours or a shift to an entirely new food item may bring relief from cerebral allergy symptoms.

Drug treatment is limited

Patients come to us with a history of many types of treatment – all futile and often toxic or even mentally retarding! Tranquillizers may be used to alter highs and anti-depressants may attenuate the lows but if these mood swings occur in a single day, how can both types of drugs be used effectively? Anti-histamines may provide sleep at night and subdue some florid symptoms during the day.

Nutritional treatment is the answer

Several vitamins are noted for their effectiveness in reducing allergic symptoms. Vitamins C and B_6 are probably the most effective. Dr William Philpott has used both of these vitamins intravenously to turn off allergic symptoms provoked by testing for allergies. The patient on adequate vitamin C will have fewer allergic symptoms. B_6 should be given to the point of nightly dream recall and the minerals calcium and potassium should be in plentiful supply in the diet. Zinc and manganese are also needed by the allergic patient. Elimination of the offending foods may be needed for several months. For multiple food allergies, in which this approach would severely limit the diet, a four-day rotation diet in which each food is eaten only once every four days should be tried. If this approach is unsuccessful, intradermal allergy testing to determine the degree of allergy and the neutralizing dose of each allergen is recommended.

Testing for allergies

Intradermal testing, which is the method we use at the Brain Bio Center, is based on reliable skin-testing procedures that are controlled, sensitive and effective methods of diagnosing food and/or inhalant allergies. Diagnosing a specific allergy consists of an intradermal injection (under the top layer of skin of the upper arm) of the food or inhalant extract in varying dilutions to determine the exact degree of sensitivity. Mild symptoms may or may not be provoked by this method. However, allergic symptoms can be reversed by a subcutaneous injection of the neutralizing or desensitizing dose. The individual would then receive neutralizing injections twice a week and would be allowed to eat foods that had been tested. For the multiple-allergic, a combination of neutralizing injections for the severe allergies and a rotation diet for the less severe is often the most practical approach.

Many different kinds of tests exist for allergies, one of which is to test the levels of proteins called immunoglobulins in the blood. A low immunoglobulin E (IgE) indicates probable inhalant allergies. Most patients with food allergies also tend to have pyroluria, a stress phenomenon associated with excess pyrroles in the urine which bind vitamin B_6 and zinc. Some allergies, such as those associated with wheat, are accompanied by damage to the intestinal mucosa (coeliac disease), resulting in the malabsorption of zinc and/or B_6, as well as other nutrients.

Reactions to everyday drugs

Allergic patients may react adversely when exposed to food dyes, aspirin, foods with salicylates, food additives, food preservatives, and the insecticides used to reduce spoilage of food. Organic food eating is therefore recommended and carefully chosen vendors become most important. Was insecticide used? Were crops sprayed? Was a preservative added? The members of one allergic family were literally driven from their home in Connecticut when the government officials decided to spray the whole landscape to kill the gypsy moths. Air deodorants and perfumes may also be offenders. In air travel one can smell the surge of deodorant wafting through the cabin at regular intervals, to the dismay and discomfort of those allergic to petrochemicals.

The ultimate outcome of careful diagnosis and treatment of the allergic patient with cerebral symptoms may be excellent. The patient must, however, watch for new allergies and follow the carefully prescribed diets and routines of avoidance.

7

The Dangers of Daily Bread

'There's a worm in the wheat . . . In stupidity street'
Ralph Hodgson (1871–1962)

Hidden sensitivity to one's daily bread may well be the cause of compulsive and ritualistic behaviour, impaired speech development and mood and behaviour changes. Not everyone can digest wheat, rye and other cereal grains. This condition is known as 'coeliac disease', and secondary symptoms may result. In coeliac disease, food may go through the gut undigested. Recent studies have indicated that coeliac disease may be responsible for many cases of 'schizophrenia'. Evidence is accumulating which links various psychiatric disturbances with malabsorption caused by cereal grains, and it is becoming increasingly apparent that for many individuals, daily bread is much less than a blessing.

Coeliac disease in childhood is a clue
One of the earliest observations of the relationship between cereal grains and schizophrenia was reported by Dr Lauretta Bender in 1953, when she noted that schizophrenic children were extraordinarily subject to coeliac disease. By 1966 she had recorded twenty such cases from among more than 2,000 schizophrenic children. In 1961 Graff and Handford published data stating that during one year, four out of thirty-seven adult male schizophrenics admitted to the Institute of Pennsylvania Hospital, Philadelphia, had a history of coeliac disease in childhood. These early observations greatly interested Dr Dohan of the Hospital of the University of Pennysylvania. He noted that these data indicated that

'schizophrenia' occurs far more frequently than chance would predict in children and also in adults with coeliac disease. Dohan believes that an inherited susceptibility to both coeliac disease and 'schizophrenia' may indeed exist and that one may contribute to the development of the other.

The signs of wheat–gluten sensitivity

The clinical symptoms of coeliac disease and 'schizophrenia' bear marked resemblance. Both physical and psychiatric symptoms are present in children and adults with coeliac disease, although the incidence of 'schizophrenia' is greater in children than in adults. Coeliac disease results in part from an impairment of food absorption from the intestine. Coeliac patients are classically very thin and have a protruding relaxed abdomen. Bowel movements are frequent and are fatty, loose, large and foul. Facial expression is typically shrivelled and drawn, suggesting a state of melancholy. In fact, the psychiatric picture of the coeliac child is not unlike that of the schizophrenic child. Both are dissociated from the world, weepy and introverted. Coeliac patients are also subject to mood disorders such as extreme depression and anxiety. These mood behaviour swings occur after cereal grain is eaten and subside when such food is carefully avoided. In adults, large blisters may occur on the skin on the back of the hands (dermatitis herpetiformis).

The toxic element which is responsible in coeliac disease is gluten, a protein found in wheat, rye, barley, and oats. The mechanisms that produce gluten intolerance have yet to be fully determined. The theory is that intestinal enzymes cannot digest the gluten and accumulating toxic material irritates the lining of the intestinal wall, causing chronic indigestion and malabsorption of all nutrients. Yet another theory suggests that 'exorphins' found in gluten compete with the body's endorphins which are vital brain chemicals involved in mood. Removal of wheat gluten and similar gluten proteins found in other cereal grains has been shown to improve digestive processes, promote weight gain, and to alleviate mood and psychiatric symptoms.

The importance of considering gluten sensitivity is well demonstrated in a study by Dr Dohan in 1969. He randomly placed all men admitted to a locked psychiatric ward in a Veterans Administration Hospital in Coatsville, Pennsylvania, either on a diet containing no milk or cereals, or on a diet that was relatively high in cereals. (Milk was eliminated from the diet because some people do not benefit when only glutens are removed.) All other treatment continued as normal. Midway through the experiment 62 per cent of the group on no milk and cereals were released to a 'full privileges' ward while only 36 per cent of those patients receiving a diet including cereal were able to leave the locked ward. When the wheat gluten was secretly placed back into the diet, the improved patients relapsed. This and subsequent studies indicate that, at present, diet is the crucial factor in treating gluten-sensitive schizophrenics. Therefore, wheat–gluten sensitivity should be considered in the pathogenesis of the 'schizophrenias', and once diagnosis has been made, patients should understand and employ a diet free from milk and cereals.

Recognizing wheat–gluten sensitivity is frequently difficult because classical symptoms are often absent. When either the doctor (or nutritionist) or the patient is even vaguely suspicious of gluten sensitivity, a special diet can be undertaken for a trial period. Weeks or months may be required before a marked improvement appears after wheat, rye, barley, oats and milk are removed from the diet. Re-introduction of these grains and milk into the diet usually produces a relapse in months, days or even hours! It is important, then, to maintain a strict adherence to the diet and to be aware of the exact ingredients of many foods.

The rewards are great
With removal of the offending foods, irritability, mood swings, compulsive behaviour and other psychiatric disorders will subside. Dr Dohan suggests that elimination diets should be tried for at least six months to a year. Further investigation is needed to determine how long the milk and cereal free diet must be followed to determine the possibility of developing a 'gluten

tolerance' which would permit careful re-introduction of these foods into the diet.

8

Hypoglycaemia – The Sugar Blues

One of the most crucial balances in the body is the blood sugar balance. Since the brain needs glucose from the blood to work properly, it is no surprise to find that hypoglycaemia (hypo = low, glyc = sugar, aemia = in the blood) and diabetes (high blood sugar) can result in the signs and symptoms of mental imbalance.

But you don't have to be mentally ill to suffer from glucose intolerance. Many people suffer those 'late afternoon blues', a syndrome which often prompts a short nap or a quick snack to revive waning energy and sinking spirits several hours before dinner. What is the cause of these unpleasant symptoms?

Just as gasoline provides the chemical energy to run an engine, sugar (glucose), manufactured from various foods and transported in the blood, is the fuel from which the body cells obtain the energy for all cellular activities. When the supply of gasoline diminishes the engine begins to splutter erratically until replenished with fuel. Similarly, body cells can no longer produce adequate energy when blood glucose and mineral stores become depleted. Of all the organs and tissues in the body, the brain is the most dependent on the minute-by-minute supply of glucose from the blood. When the blood sugar level drops, the brain immediately suffers, resulting in fatigue and emotional chaos.

Are you glucose intolerant?

Do you have disperceptions and

1. Weakness, fatigue, faintness and dizziness
2. Nervousness, irritability, trembling and anxiety
3. Depression, forgetfulness, confusion and difficulty concentrating
4. Palpitations or blackouts

If so you will benefit from:

1. Avoidance of the junk foods, sugar, alcohol, and white bread
2. Regular exercise
3. Manganese (as gluconate) 10mg a.m. and p.m.
4. Zinc, 15mg, a.m. and p.m.
5. B_3 + Chromium (GTF), a.m. and p.m.
6. A multivitamin tablet (without copper)

Defining hypoglycaemia

Low blood sugar, technically termed hypoglycaemia, is usually responsible for those late-afternoon blues. It represents a chemical change in the body due to a decrease in immediately available glucose. This chemical change occurs in every person several times a day. Although hypoglycaemia *per se* is not a disease, in recent times the term has become synonymous with chronic low blood sugar, a disease state resulting from an error in the body's regulation of blood glucose levels because of inadequate minerals. The lacking minerals are calcium, magnesium, potassium, phosphate and the trace elements manganese, zinc and chromium.

Balancing blood sugar

Blood glucose levels depend on the action of a number of inter-related factors. Ingested foods are converted into various substances by enzymes in the gut. Glucose can be manufactured from protein, fats and carbohydrates, but carbohydrates are most rapidly and commonly converted to glucose. A short time after a meal, glucose manufactured in the gut enters the blood-stream. Cells within the hypothalamus (a part of the brain) detect this transient high blood sugar concentration and initiate a series of biochemical re-adjustments. Signals from hypothalamic cells trigger the pancreas (a somewhat elongated organ situated below the stomach) to secrete insulin.

Insulin gets sugar into cells

Insulin is a hormone which promotes rapid absorption of glucose from the body by the cells of various tissues in the body. Insulin greatly helps the transport of glucose into liver cells. As glucose passes into the liver cells it is converted into glycogen, for storage. Each molecule of insulin released from the pancreas aids in the removal of thousands of glucose molecules from the blood into the cells.

When the blood glucose concentration decreases considerably, hypothalamic cells in the brain signal the pituitary to stimulate the adrenal glands to release adrenalin and the glucocorticoid hormones which antagonize insulin activity. Adrenalin antagonizes the action of insulin by promoting a specific enzymatic activity in cells throughout the body which blocks glucose uptake. Adrenalin and the glucocorticoid hormones also trigger the pancreas to secrete glucagon (another hormone) which, in turn, promotes the conversion of glycogen to glucose in the liver. The liberated glucose is then released from the liver into the blood-stream.

Sugar cannot be stored or used without minerals

Many vitamins and trace elements, including vitamin C, the B complex of vitamins, calcium, potassium, magnesium, zinc, chromium, manganese and phosphorus, are involved in glucose metabolism and the activities of the endocrine glands. The recently discovered Glucose Tolerance Factor (GTF) which contains chromium, B_3 and three amino acids, is essential for the proper functioning of insulin and is necessary for proper carbohydrate metabolism. Brewer's yeast is the best known natural source of GTF.

When any of the mechanisms involved in blood glucose regulation becomes affected by disease or begins functioning poorly, the result is a lack of balance between glucose, insulin and insulin antagonists. If too much insulin and/or too few insulin antagonists are produced, the result is chronic low blood sugar.

Testing for glucose intolerance

Hair analysis is probably the most versatile of the diagnostic tests. At the time of writing, it costs less than £20. If you eat junk food, the body runs low on zinc, manganese and chromium, and other minerals such as calcium and magnesium are mobilized to use and store the excess glucose. The hair of the purely nutritionally hypoglycaemic patient will therefore show high calcium and magnesium with low zinc, manganese and chromium. However, other dietary indiscretions such as high copper or low potassium may obscure this finding.

For around £40, you can have an oral five-hour glucose tolerance test. This method involves fasting for twelve hours, then ingesting glucose. At hourly or half-hourly intervals a blood sample is taken and tested for glucose levels. This will usually disclose nutritional hypoglycaemia, diabetes and pre-diabetic states.

At the Brain Bio Center, you can get a blood level of histamine, spermidine, and spermine, three useful markers of possible biochemical imbalance. Histamine provides the answer to histapenia or histadelia, spermidine is an indicator of rapid cell growth, and spermine, when low, indicates nutritional hypoglycaemia.

A high complex carbohydrate diet works best

Nutritionists and nutritionally-oriented doctors have traditionally prescribed a high protein, low carbohydrate diet for their hypoglycaemic patients, with an emphasis on frequent meals and snacks. Such a diet often included large quantities of animal protein, and excluded carbohydrate-containing foods such as whole grains and fruits. Today we know that a diet low in animal protein, but high in complex carbohydrates gives consistently better results. The key is the emphasis on *complex* carbohydrates – not the pure white sugar so many people find addictive, but the type of carbohydrates found in vegetables, nuts, seeds, whole grains (such as oatmeal) and potatoes. When used as the core of the hypoglycaemic diet, these naturally occurring carbohydrates help regulate blood sugar levels, thus preventing the rapid swings responsible for hypoglycaemic symptoms. These whole foods also contain the trace minerals necessary for the transport and utilization of carbohydrates once inside the body.

Other causes for hypoglycaemia
Impaired glucose metabolism engendered by disease is classified as organic or fasting hypoglycaemia, since symptoms become more pronounced when food is withheld. An insulin secreting tumour of the pancreatic islet cells (the cells which make insulin) produces severe fasting hypoglycaemia. Congenital liver enzyme defects, damage to the liver produced by alcohol, tobacco or infection, encephalitis, brain tumours, hypopituitarism and Addison's disease (an exhaustion of the adrenal gland) also cause hypoglycaemia. All of these are rare diseases, accounting for only a few of the hypoglycaemic disorders.

Defects in glucose metabolism resulting from secondary factors occur with far greater frequency. Such disorders are classified as nutritional, functional, reactive or fed hypoglycaemia, because symptoms develop in response to food intake. Alimentary hypoglycaemia, one type of nutritional glycaemia, often develops in patients who undergo subtotal gastrectomy for peptic ulcers, as foods pass more rapidly into the small intestine when part of the stomach has been removed. Most often, however, prolonged stress, particularly the internal disturbance provoked by poor eating habits, precipitates hypoglycaemia.

Stress releases blood sugar and minerals
Any physical or emotional trauma, such as pain, over-exertion,

childbearing, anxiety, grief, or fear, causes the adrenal gland to release adrenalin, prompting an increase in blood glucose to supply the extra energy needed to deal with the stress. When a person suffers continual stress, the adrenal gland must constantly supply adrenalin. Eventually, this persistent demand exhausts the adrenal gland. When challenged, it can no longer produce enough adrenalin and hypoglycaemia results.

Sugar provides empty calories

Nutritionally inadequate foods, without trace elements, exert a subtle, but complex and damaging stress on the body's regulation of glucose metabolism. Refined carbohydrates are the worst offenders.

Sucrose, the refined sugar in baked goods, sweets and the sugar bowl, consists of a molecule of glucose and a molecule of fructose. When sugar is eaten, enzymes in the small intestine readily break the bond between the two simple sugars and glucose with fructose surges into the blood-stream, signalling the pancreas to release batallions of insulin molecules. Insulin rapidly admits glucose to the cells and the level of glucose in the blood quickly decreases. This action is responsible for the quick but temporary energy provided by a bar of chocolate.

Empty calories stress the pancreas and adrenal glands

When repeatedly forced to handle large amounts of glucose (derived from a diet rich in refined sugars), the pancreas becomes sensitized and hypoglycaemia develops. Every time glucose enters the blood, the pancreas over-reacts, releasing too much insulin which causes the cells to absorb and utilize glucose at top speed. The adrenal gland, striving to maintain the proper glucose level, becomes exhausted. Soon after a meal, blood sugar falls below the fasting levels and the body craves sugar, producing hypoglycaemia symptoms. Another dose of sugar relieves symptoms for a short time, so many hypoglycaemics nibble continually on sweets, without minerals, a pattern which only aggravates the underlying metabolic disorder.

Too much sugar

Increased consumption of refined carbohydrates during the past fifty years probably accounts for the rising incidence of diabetes and hypoglycaemia in recent times. In the 19th century, the per capita intake of sugar in England was only 7 pounds per person per year. Today, people in England, and in western countries as a whole, consume as much as 128 pounds of sugar per year and the human body cannot adapt to this drastic change.

Mark Twain once advised that the 'secret to success in life is to eat what you like and let the food fight it out inside', but this statement came some time before the present avalanche of sugary foods reached the market. Today, most people eat to satisfy their sweet tooth with refined carbohydrates, and the food is indeed 'fighting it out inside' – in many cases wholly defeating the glucose regulatory mechanisms. Doctors specializing in metabolic disorders estimate that at least one in twenty people suffer from hypoglycaemia.

Governments advise dramatic reduction in sugar intake

Both the US Senate Select Committee and the government sponsored National Advisory Committee on Nutrition Education (NACNE) report advise a halving of average sugar consumption. But since sugar is cheap, mildly addictive (and there are many sugar addicts about) and extends the shelf life of many foods, it is little wonder that the food industry even puts 30 per cent sugar into ketchup and 23 per cent into sauces and salad dressings. There is no doubt that these sugar-rich convenience foods are making more and more people hypoglycaemic.

What are the symptoms?

When cells utilize available glucose so rapidly that the blood cannot readily meet the constant demand for more fuel, the cells actually become starved. Glucose deficiency drastically alters the function of the brain, since the brain cells cannot store glucose and thus require a continuous supply to generate energy. In a state of glucose starvation, the brain suffers reduced efficiency and can no longer completely direct vital processes, thus disrupting physical and emotional behaviour.

Physical and emotional disturbances in the hypoglycaemic disorders vary according to the severity of the disorder and the individual affected. Mental symptoms frequently resulting from hypoglycaemia include fatigue, irritability, nervousness, depression and crying spells, vertigo or dizziness, faintness, insomnia, mental confusion or forgetfulness, inability to concentrate, anxiety, phobias and fears, disperceptions, disruptive outbursts, and headaches. Such symptoms are non-specific and are present in many disorders, but strongly indicate hypoglycaemia when they occur from time to time, after fasting, late at night, first thing in the morning, or in direct relation to the time or content of a meal.

Low blood pressure and low body temperature

A distinctive characteristic of hypoglycaemia is low blood pressure and lowered body temperature. Hypoglycaemics often complain of cold hands and feet and many experience cold sweats. Dr Freinkel (1972) and Dr Molar (1974) studied hypothermia in laboratory-induced hypoglycaemia and found significant decreases in body temperature associated with the onset of other hypoglycaemic symptoms. Both doctors attribute this phenomenon to the effect of glucose deficiency on brain cells, since the hypothalamus controls body temperature. Many doctors note the low blood pressure but shrug it off with 'Well, you'll never die of high blood pressure'. A normal blood pressure is needed to keep the hands warm and the mind alert. Manganese raises blood pressure and all hypoglycaemic patients are deficient in manganese.

Hypoglycaemia is easy to treat

For many 'diseases of lifestyle' the outlook is grim but not so for hypoglycaemia. All that is needed for the disease to go away is a change in lifestyle. A change to a 'caveman's diet', high in complex carbohydrate, together with daily exercise will not only do away with some symptoms but also make all the tests go negative – to such an extent that the hospital doctor may say, 'See your glucose tolerance test is normal, you never had that mystical disease called hypoglycaemia!' You should know better since you have cured yourself by eating the foods with natural minerals, by taking proper mineral and vitamin supplements, and by exercising to your tolerance each day.

9

Minerals, Mood Swings and Manic Depression

Without a doubt, some families have relatives who seasonally get the blues or fly so high in their moods that they literally give away their home. If the high mood is controllable they work day and night and make enough money to afford to spend their depressed moods in a luxury hotel. There the doctor in residence eventually gets to know the whole family and gives encouragement and appropriate treatment. As time passes, the elevated productive mood returns and the victim of manic-depression goes back to work. Compared to other mental disorders the manic-depressive mood change is rather noble since we remember the mood changes in the kings of Shakespeare's tragedies. This illness occurs most often in colour-blind males who also have O-type blood. Like haemophilia, the disorder is linked to the X chromosome, so many women are carriers of the disorder. Manic-depression was presumably not adequately named so psychiatrists introduced the useless term 'bi-polar disorder' for the manic-depressive patient. Those who only get depressed periodically are now labelled 'mono-polar disorder' patients.

Understanding cyclical mood changes

The most common mood change is that which occurs daily. Some people learn early in life that they are 'morning larks', while others do their best work at night and are 'night owls'. These pairs make unlikely room-mates and equally mismatched mates in marriage. The morning cup of caffeine (tea or coffee) will chase the morning blues and overdosage may produce jitters and manic behaviour. If mood changes are not owing to drug intake (caffeine, alcohol, cocaine), then the possibility of food allergy or hypoglycaemia should be carefully investigated. Dr Walter Alvarez, in the 1920s, first found that his blue Mondays occurred because his family were rich enough to have chicken every Sunday. When he avoided chicken on Sunday, his Mondays were once again productive. Thus daily or even day-to-day mood changes are almost always due to food allergies or hypoglycaemia. Some patients are affected by the sun and feel better at night, when the sun is behind the earth. They get jobs as cooks in all-night restaurants or sort the cheques for the banks at night.

Weekly mood changes can be correlated with the work pattern of a seven-day week. Many migraine patients have depression and headaches at the weekend. This is called relaxation headache, and the migraine sufferer may therefore never get to rest and evolves into the 'Type A' personality that seldom relaxes – the workaholic. Excessive stress may dissipate all zinc and B_6 so that the person becomes pyroluric and has excessive mood swings. Most of the patients who come to the Brain Bio Center with a diagnosis of manic-depression and have weekly swings in mood are merely pyroluric. They are easily treated with adequate zinc and B_6. Monthly mood changes can be correlated with hormonal changes in the female and moon phases in both sexes. Much has been written about pre-menstrual tension, but it is not generally known that the tension occurs when blood copper is highest and the blood zinc is lowest. Copper is a stimulant to the brain, while zinc has an anti-anxiety effect. This metal imbalance reverses at the onset of menstruation, often coinciding with relief of tension and other symptoms. Much has been written about the lunar (moon) effect from which we originally got the word 'lunacy' and 'lunatic'. One only has to consider the powerful effect the moon has in creating tides to realize that each one of us (we are, after all, 66 per cent water) is also affected by the moon.

Seasonal changes in mood are well known. Peptic ulcers tend to be activated in the spring and autumn, inhalant allergy is more common in the spring with trees and grass pollen, and in the autumn with weed pollens. The allergic patients learn early in life about seasonal tormentors. Springtime is a period of increased energy and growth in the northern hemisphere so appropriate stresses and bodily changes are to be expected.

Some patients are depressed during their entire life. These patients are either deficient in thyroid function or high in histamine, or both. A trial of thyroid usually allows them to get over their daily depression. A blood analysis for the histamine level or a basophil count will establish the presence of a high level of blood histamine. The avoidance of folic acid and the use of daily methionine (an amino acid) will dispel their daily depression.

Lithium – an effective treatment for mania

Lithium therapy for over-excited patients was discovered in 1949 by Dr John Cade of Australia, but medical acceptance has been slow. For instance, lithium therapy for the treatment only of the manic stage of manic-depressive disorders was started in 1970. Because of the excellent studies of a Danish investigator, Dr Schau, lithium therapy has been available since 1960 in Denmark and other countries. Numerous publications have appeared indicating that lithium therapy is also useful in the treatment of chronic depression, alcoholism, pre-menstrual depression, and hyperthyroidism.

Dr Manfred Anke, of the Karl Marx Veterinary School of Leipzig, Germany, has found that lithium is an essential element needed by the goat and the miniature pig. (This discovery, if extended to man, may mean that psychiatrists who prescribe lithium are, unwittingly, meganutrient therapists!) Lithium-deficient animals lie dormant with no muscle tone. This finding needs to be confirmed since we have many patients who have only a trace of lithium in their hair and may therefore benefit from supplementing lithium.

We have used lithium in schizophrenic and other patients for a period of fifteen years. We know that lithium has no effect on hallucinations, but lithium does allow the non-hallucinatory patient to reduce his effective anti-psychotic drug dose. The side effects of large doses of Prolixin are therefore diminished. The patient is also better able to tolerate hallucinations while on lithium therapy.

Lithium is specific, according to Dr Levy. 'The patient receiving lithium treatment is alert without lethargy or sedation. It seems clear that lithium is the ideal therapeutic agent for acute and chronic mania. It is also very effective for the hypomanic states whose frequent recurrence leads to deterioration of the patient's social situation. In this type of patient, lithium is superior to other drugs which produce only brief symptomatic improvement and a large amount of sedation.'

Low doses of lithium can relieve depression

What has caused even more interest in lithium is that it appears to be active as a prophylactic agent against recurrent psychotic depression. Studies have shown that lithium given on an ongoing basis in smaller does to patients with recurrent depression is able to substantially diminish the depressive attacks. The fact holds true whether the patient has shown only depression in the past or has had alternating phases of mania and depression. If used on a regular basis, lithium requires a dosage with few side-effects and causes no restriction of normal emotional expression.

Some professionals motivated by inexperience (and their desire to fill hospital beds) tell the patient that 'Lithium therapy can only be started in a hospital where daily lithium levels will be run.' This is untrue! We, and others, have found that patients between the ages of 12 and 50 years can be started on two 300mg tablets of lithium carbonate per day, and the lithium level can be determined at monthly intervals. Patients frequently do well on only two tablets of lithium per day. (The mean lithium level produced by this low dose therapy is 0.4 meg/1. The recommended therapeutic level for mania is 0.5-1.5 meg/1. Therefore, we are well below the level that might produce any untoward reaction). We sometimes suggest that the patient, if unimproved, start lithium therapy (two tablets per day) two weeks before the next scheduled visit. We then do a blood serum lithium level.

What are the side-effects?

The side-effects depend on the dosage used. One or two tablets or capsules per day (American tablets contain 300mg lithium carbonate; European contain 400mg) may produce a fine tremor of the hands, slight tiredness and sleepiness. Three to four tablets or capsules a day can bring on nausea, diarrhoea, increased thirst and urination, and low thyroid function.

Lithium is compatible with all of the tranquillizers, vitamins, nutrients, and antibiotics when the dose is small. Some reports indicate that haloperidol (Haldol) and lithium provide a sometimes lethal combination when given in large doses. This is true of any major tranquillizer with large doses of lithium. Lithium shouldn't be recommended for patients on digitalis or diuretic pills.

Advantages of lithium therapy

Because lithium is excreted slowly from the body, this means that a therapeutic level is maintained longer and also allows simple blood tests for lithium to determine whether the patient is sticking to the treatment. At high levels lithium causes nausea and vomiting, which means that patients are unlikely to overdose. In conjunction with good nutrition, lithium is a viable alternative to the more dangerous drugs commonly used for manic-depressed and chronically depressed people.

10

Diet, Crime and Delinquency

In America and in Britain the incidence of violent, psychopathic and anti-social behaviour is rapidly rising. Prisons are full and the cost of keeping so many people in prison is becoming unmanageable and expensive. But what is the solution?

Perhaps even more depressing than the need for further research into schizophrenia is the need for a research institute dealing with psychopathic, violent or anti-social behaviour. An institute is really needed here because out-patient help is impossible when dealing with violent and psychopathic individuals.

There is little doubt that nutritional and biochemical imbalances play a large part in behaviour disorders. We know of at least nine biochemical imbalances which can result in violent behaviour. These are, in their probable order of importance, the following:

1. Pyroluria (combined zinc and B_6 deficiency due to the mauve factor in the urine).

2. Hypoglycaemia (and deficiency of manganese due to the eating of junk foods or empty calories).

3. Histadelia – high histamine levels in the blood. (This characterizes the addictive person.)

4. Excess copper (or other metals) and histadelia.

5. Cerebral allergy (usually milk, wheat or corn).

6. Increased testosterone can lead to rape. Treated with progesterone injections.

7. Psychomotor epilepsy attacks (cerebellar stimulation helps).

8. XYY Syndrome – excessive height and violence in males.

9. Pre-menstrual syndrome (PMS), coupled with zinc, magnesium and vitamin B_6 deficiency.

Most of these bio-types can easily be diagnosed and treated by our known remedies. The stumbling block at present is the lack of trained personnel and a laboratory to perform the tests accurately.

Diet and behaviour

Books have been written on the subject of diet and its links with behaviour. There can be no doubt that a diet high in sugar, additives and stimulants like coffee, and low in nutrients is associated with anti-social behaviour. So the very first step is to reduce sugar and junk food intake by inmates and patients. Education is so often the key, and the establishment of prison nutrition clubs to promote awareness of good nutrition among patients, prisoners and security personnel, backed up by the availability of food charts and literature, would do much to improve the awareness so sadly lacking. The next step would be the gradual establishment of diagnostic centres at each prison and hospital.

11

How to Age Without Senility

Senility is described as a 'mental disease in which brain cells cease to function properly, resulting in a deficit in memory and mental capability'. The size of the problem is on the increase. One in four people over 75, and one in seven over 65, are classified as senile. In fact, a third of all hospital beds are filled with geriatrics, a large proportion of them institutionalized because of senility. The cost to the taxpayer runs into billions.

What is senility?
To understand senility we must examine the nature of memory. In a lifetime, more than 15 trillion specific memories are coded in our brain. Although much of what we perceive is forgotten, selected glimpses remain permanently etched, waiting for recall.

So memory can be divided into short-term (lasting a few seconds or minutes) or long-term. Computer scientists estimate that it would require a modern computer the size of Buckingham Palace to hold the information in our cabbage-sized brains. How do we hold this information? And what goes wrong?

Two theories
Two current theories exist. One involves coding through lipoproteins, fat-containing proteins in the brain. In fact, every cell in our brain contains special kinds of fat, which can be synthesized only from the essential fatty acids, linoleic and linolenic acid. Synthesis of these is made even easier by the intake

of fatty fish, high in EPA, or evening primrose oil, high in gamma-linolenic acid.

The other theory is based on coding through RNA, the messenger molecule in charge of building new cells. Since most of the brain cells are replaced within twenty-four hours, the clue to memory must be transmittable. Foods high in RNA, like fish, have been shown to boost mental activity and memory in animals.

Research at the Brain Bio Center has revealed a link between senile dementia and the polyamine spermine – which the brain badly needs to make more RNA. The minerals zinc and, most importantly, manganese help to bring low spermine levels back to normal.

What exactly goes wrong with those suffering from senile dementia? One common finding is that premature senile dementia, known as Alzheimer's disease, is an entanglement of nerve fibres. When these nerve clusters are found in the frontal and temporal regions of the brain they are frequently loaded with aluminium. It is highly likely that our involuntary consumption of aluminium contributes to deteriorating memory and mental performance. We get aluminium from cooking utensils and food packaging, including aluminium foil. People with indigestion risk an extra dose from many types of antacids.

Another hypothesis is that the nerve cells are simply not getting enough blood. The brain uses a fifth of your blood supply. Most people by the age of 50 have a degree of arteriosclerosis and atherosclerosis – hardening and 'furring up' of the arteries. In severe cases this leads to a stroke, where the whole blood supply to a portion of the brain is cut off. The result is death or partial paralysis.

When cells are starved of oxygen they switch to a more primitive mode of operation called anaerobic respiration. The cells begin to divide and spread – unless they are nerve cells, that is, because nerve cells can't regenerate. So what happens to them? They just stop working. The result is senility.

Oxygen boosters

To keep cells running on oxygen requires much more than a good blood supply. Vitamins are also involved in the process of oxygen and energy metabolism. The most important are vitamins B_1 and B_3 and the antioxidant nutrients C, E and selenium.

B_1 deficiency has long been known to result in brain damage. One of the most dangerous problems of excessive alcohol consumption is induced B_1 deficiency. The condition is called Wernicke-Korsakof syndrome. The symptoms include anxiety and depression, obsessive thinking, confusion, defective memory (especially for recent events) and time distortion – not so different from senility.

Vitamin B_3, also known as nicotinic acid or nicotinamide, is crucial for oxygen utilization. It is incorporated into the coenzyme NAD (nicotinamide adenosine dinucleotide), and many reactions involving oxygen need NAD. Without it, pellagra and senility can develop.

Memory boosters

Other memory boosters include B vitamins, especially choline. This nutrient probably works by boosting the levels of acetylcholine, an important nerve transmitter substance. In studies at the Palo Alto hospital in California, drugs which boost acetylcholine induced 'supermemories'. Choline on its own is effective in improving short-term and long-term memory, but the doses have to be high (10 grams a day) and the effects aren't very long lasting. Pantothenic acid, B_5, is also important in acetylcholine synthesis. Deanol is a more effective choline derivative which easily passes all membrane barriers. The dose is only 100mg per day, rather than 10g as with choline.

Optimum nutrition

But don't the elderly get enough of these vital vitamins? Sadly, the answer is an unequivocal 'no'. And anyway enough isn't always enough. Dr Abram Hoffer has shown that when cells have been starved of these nutrients they may become vitamin dependent, requiring many hundred times the normal daily requirements.

One study in the States in 1975 failed to find a single geriatric patient with a normal nutritional profile! The most common deficiencies were C, E, A and B_3.

Other studies have found the elderly to be frequently deficient in folic acid, zinc, iron and of course calcium. To prevent the risk of heart and artery disease many researchers have recommended low-fat diets, cutting down on dairy produce and meat. This often leads to even worse iron, zinc and calcium status, unless proper dietary guidance and supplementation is given. Many elderly people have impaired sense of taste, leading to over-salting of food.

With optimum nutrition I believe senility and memory deterioration will become a thing of the past. As Leonard Larson, president of the American Medical Association in 1960, said, 'There are no diseases of the aged, but simply diseases among the aged.'

12

Drugs – The Treatment That Leads Nowhere

Since the 1950s the treatment of mental illness with drugs has become the major therapeutic tool of psychiatrists the world over. The first anti-psychotic drug, reserpine, was introduced into psychiatric practice in 1952, shortly followed by chlorpromazine (Thorazine) in 1954. The perfecting of this type of anti-psychotic drug was achieved in the 1960s with the introduction of Fluphenazine (Prolixin) and haloperidol (Haldol). Most other drugs introduced since 1970 have been 'me too' drugs which have little advantage over these two standard and now cheaper drugs. For patients who will not co-operate on the taking of medication by mouth, the oil-soluble decanoate salts are available for intra-muscular injection. These weekly injections – for example, of Depixol – do not give as smooth a result as the daily use of the drug by mouth. Most patients can have the daily dose they need given by mouth at bedtime with diphenhydramine (Benadryl). If an antidote to any muscle shakes (side action) is needed, Cogentin or Artane can be given in a small dose each morning.

Drugs such as the major tranquillizers should be considered as temporary crutches which can be used until the biochemical imbalances are slowly corrected by nutrient therapy. Anti-psychotic drugs, if continued at high doses for many months, may produce tardive dyskinesia – a delayed impairment of voluntary motion causing incomplete or partial movement. Manganese taken daily in doses of 50mg is helpful, as is the daily use of Deanol which builds up acetylcholine, the normal working hormone in muscle contraction.

Another problem is multiple drug interactions. Many psychiatric patients take, simultaneously, daily doses of one or more anti-psychotics, anti-depressants, a minor tranquillizer and a hypnotic to make them sleep at night. In addition, because of certain side-effects of these drugs, which resemble the symptoms of Parkinson's disease, most patients are given an atropine-like drug (anti-Parkinson agent) such as Artane or Cogentin. These make the reading of the printed page even more difficult. Then there are drugs for co-existing illnesses prescribed by other doctors and self-medication with over-the-counter drugs, all of which the patient could conceivably take simultaneously. All this adds up to a potentially dangerous constellation of pharmacological inter-action and personal neglect of the patient which might prolong suffering and delay rehabilitation.

Studies have indicated that only a few patients on anti-psychotic drugs require an anti-Parkinson drug for a prolonged period. And while anti-psychotic drugs can have great beneficial effects, the lethargic, asocial, odd behaviour of some patients, which is usually attributed to illness, may well be the result of medication. In these patients, when dosages are reduced or drugs discontinued, a favourable transformation occurs, the patients become more social and much of the odd behaviour disappears.

Often the wrong drugs are recommended. There are many reasons why this could occur, such as understaffing in hospitals, lack of interaction between patient and doctor, discrepancies between scientific understanding and clinical use, and the effects of drug advertising, which doesn't always serve the best interests of responsible medical practice. Whatever the cause, it is important that the patient knows there are viable alternatives from which to choose. Adequate diagnosis combined with an improvement of diet and treatment with specific nutrients are the first steps towards a more effective and tolerable treatment. If needed, a drug such as haloperidol or fluphenazine may be substituted for chlorpromazine. These produce fewer side-effects and can be used as 'holding drugs' until the nutrients begin to take effect. A 'pharmacological lobotomy' is not at all necessary, nor is the frustrating disruption of patients' imaginative resources.

The danger of long-term drug use

Prolonged use of haloperidol or fluphenazine (without extra nutrients) can result in tardive dyskinesia. The nutrients which will help prevent this chronic illnes are manganese with choline or Deanol which, as we have already seen, is a precursor for acetylcholine, an important neurotransmitter. Once the disorder has appeared, the use of choline, Deanol and manganese may take weeks or months to correct the abnormal movements caused by tardive dyskinesia.

The 'neuroleptic malignant syndrome' is yet another sometimes lethal side-effect of anti-schizophrenic medication. More than twenty publications have depicted the sad effects of prolonged use of the anti-schizophrenic drugs. Patients may get elevated temperature, sweating, rapid pulse, panting, soiling, rigidity, dazed mutism, stupor and coma. If the drug is not withdrawn, death can occur within twenty-four hours.

Drugs can have serious side-effects

A problem which has been overlooked in the treatment of mental disorders until recently is the discomfort to the patient resulting from the side-effects of some psychotherapeutic drugs. Drugs such as the now antiquated chlorpromazine, (Thorazine or Largactil) can have some annoying and sometimes serious side-effects. Patients taking these drugs may find themselves unable to steady their hands; their facial muscles may twitch involuntarily; they may try to read but find their vision is too blurred to decipher the printed lines. The eyes may turn up and refuse to come down. The patients may be restless and pace the floor until they have blistered feet. A severe skin reaction may follow even a brief exposure to the sun so that patients on the drug are compelled to spend much of their time indoors. After long-term drug therapy a patient may look in the mirror one morning to discover that his face has acquired a purplish-grey hue, a very slowly reversible condition. This pigment is also in the heart muscle and may cause

Figure 5. Drugs: the door that leads nowhere.

sudden death, as several studies have shown. An intelligent young man or woman, particularly the artistic or intellectual type, may make the frustrating discovery that their much-valued imaginative facilities are no longer available. Is it ethical, twenty-five years after the introduction of chlorpromazine, to increase the agony of the suffering schizophrenic by giving him this drug when safer drugs are available?

With newer and better drugs, and improved methods of treating the schizophrenias through nutrition, any informed medical doctor should know that chlorpromazine is antiquated. Yet some psychiatric consultants will prescribe it only because it is the oldest tranquillizer.

Even today, many public mental hospitals are grossly understaffed and lack badly needed funds. One unfortunate consequence of this inadequacy is that excessive doses of chlorpromazine are routinely prescribed to keep the patient quiet. Medical supervision is minimal and treatment isn't monitored properly. Chlorpromazine is also cheaper, which appeals to the economy-minded purchasing agent of the hospital.

Adequate diagnosis, improvement of the diet and treatment with specific nutrients is the first step toward a more effective and tolerable treatment.

13

Why Nutrition is The Way Forward

At a Scientific Congress in May 1985 at Dallas, Texas, a British psychiatrist said that it only took two years of double blind studies* to establish the positive action of chlorpromazine in schizophrenics. Why were we so slow in doing double blind studies with nutrients? I countered that it takes only two minutes to establish the mind-blowing effect of cocaine!

Nutrients don't have side-effects

Drugs are different from nutrients. Drugs are like sky rockets, a magic display, a big bang – then a baneful burn-out. Nutrients are like the 'little engine that could', climbing a hill. The patient improves slowly, 'I think I can, I think I am better, I am better, I knew I could, I've never felt better'. Of course, there's occasional slipping of the drive wheels but no big bang and baneful burn-out. Only slow but steady progress towards normality. Nutrients seldom produce an artificial high. The neurotic who wants a speed effect to equal cocaine or the amphetamines is disappointed in the effects of the nutrients. Drugs are foreign to the body's natural biochemistry and thus produce side-effects. Nutrients are part of us so side-effects are minimal and seldom lethal. The nutrients such as vitamins, amino acids and trace elements have existed ever

*In a double blind study one group of patients are given the real drug or nutrient and the other group are given a dummy pill. The groups must be identical. Neither the researcher nor the patient is allowed to know who is in which group to exclude the risk of bias.

since cells began to congregate to form tissues and tissues organize to form skin glands, muscles, bones and nerves. These nutrients were in beneficial biochemical action before any minds began to form thoughts or tongues touched teeth to speak soft words, 'I'm hungry Mum!'

Trace elements have been acting as intelligent ions for eons long before scientists discovered their actions. They and other nutrients know exactly where to go in the body and what to do. They don't have to be infused into the brain by means of a thin catheter and an implanted pump. Such drug studies make newspaper headlines with great publicity but little biochemical sense.

The 'psychosomatic' diagnosis is a dead end

With the nutritional approach to disease, the known blood or tissue levels and biochemical actions of each individual nutrient provide opportunities for objective measurement, the necessary yardsticks for calculating the degree of impairment of the body and the slow gradual improvement which occurs as the nutrients speed up normal biochemical processes. These objective signs are the keys to disease, from which we can learn exactly what is going on. I recall examining a psychiatrist at the University of Illinois who was defending a master's thesis entitled 'A Case of Narcolepsy of Psychological Origin'. Narcolepsy is characterized by a sudden onset of involuntary sleep and we now know so much about narcolepsy that the psychosomatic label is seldom applied or even contemplated. A member of the committee, the late Warren McCullough MD, was wise. He said, 'I am willing to admit that your case of narcolepsy might be psychosomatic in origin but if you had 1,000 similar cases, what in your work-up or diagnosis would let you say that one case among the 1,000 was not of psychosomatic origin? Perhaps you are guided by Sigmund Freud's theories. If you apply his teachings what would make you say that 1 in 1,000 or 1 in 100,000 is not of psychological origin?' The candidate couldn't answer and blurted out, 'I don't think there is a psychiatrist in Chicago, Dr McCullough, who could answer your question.' Dr McCullough was right. The exceptions always prove the rule, so that without objective data it is impossible to say whether a disease is of psychological or physical origin. So often, people suffering from real diseases are passed on to the psychiatrist for a waste-basket diagnosis of 'psychosomatic origin'. Man has an excellent brain for continuous observation of many objective findings. The exquisite senses of the investigator should seldom be obscured by double blind tests.

For example, Dr Warren McCullough served in the British Navy aboard a submarine in the First World War. The watch changed every four hours and the men slept in hammocks. At the change of the watch, the watch orderly blew a bugle at close quarters to awaken the men. The older sailors would simply put one leg out of their hammocks in response to this strong stimulus, but did not awaken; the watch orderly would then hit the bottom of the hammocks with a paddle in an attempt to awaken the sailors who were still asleep; when that failed, he would cut the rope to the hammocks and let the sailors fall to the deck. These old sailors were indeed sound sleepers but when the skipper changed the course of the submarine in the middle of the night, the same sailors would awaken and yell 'Why did he change the direction of the submarine?' For them that subtle stimulus was stronger than the bugle!

The story of young Carl Frederick Gauss (1792–1870), the mathematical genius, is another example of man's excellent brain. At school one day, the teacher needed a breather to plan her work, so she said to the class, 'You will take your slates and add all the numbers from 1 to 100'. Busy work indeed! After two minutes young Gauss raised his hand and said, 'I have the answer to your problem of adding a large string of numbers. It occurs to me that 1 plus 100 is 101, that 99 plus 2 is 101, and that 98 plus 3 is 101. Therefore, this makes 50 pairs of numbers and the answer to your problem is 50 × 101. Using this formula I can easily add the numbers from 1 to 1,000!' The mathematical brain of young Gauss was fantastic!

As another example, in the early days of the telegraph the

operators discovered that they could reliably distinguish the telegraph key and the operators by delicate changes in sound and rhythm. The acme of diagnosis occurred when the New York City operator had a perplexed frown on his face. When questioned he stated, 'Most unusual, indeed. It's the Washington telegraph operator working the Wilmington telegraph key.' This recognition of the hand on the key was used in the First World War and is still used to determine if the brave soldier behind the enemy lines is the one who was sent with the telegraph key to give information on troop movements.

The human ear is an exquisitely sensitive radar scope that automatically turns the head in the direction of the source of sound. The human voice in normal individuals modulates according to the distance of the listener. This personal space is upset in mental disease, usually in the direction of inappropriate loudness.

By the objective tests referred to in this book, many types of mental illness can be properly identified. These objective criteria are hand-holds or clues that should be followed in the treatment of diseases.

'Double blind' research isn't the only way

Despite all the findings, many medical scientists of today only believe results from 'double-blind' studies. But because of the narrow statistical training of many research scientists, the keys to disease are usually ignored in double blind tests. Many absurd studies have been done doubly blind. For example, we know that many zinc-deficient teenagers have acne. Zinc dietary supplements benefit acne. Zinc is a natural nutrient which is needed by the body. A broad-spectrum antibiotic also benefits acne. So what happened? A group of skin specialists tested, in a double blind fashion, zinc against tetracycline in a fixed dose schedule. Under these circumstances the tetracycline proved to be significantly better for acne. But the zinc is needed by the body while the tetracycline is not. What's more, tetracycline reduces the resistance to some fungal infections like candida. The ideal goal in acne is a zero blood level of tetracycline and adequate zinc. Yet the dose of zinc needed by each individual was not determined!

In Ireland, there is a high incidence of spina bifida babies among malnourished women, probably because of a nutrient deficiency in which the vitamin folic acid is known to be low. The use of vitamin supplements has decreased the incidence of spina bifida.

As reported by Nim Barnes, Dr Smithells from England has convincing evidence that folic acid and other nutrients are needed by the mother at the time of conception. The Beecham company which provided the multivitamin preparation refused to conduct or supply vitamins for a randomized double blind study in which more spina bifida or other neural tube defective babies would be born. This is not altruism. They just don't want to be sued. To us it's also common sense to refuse a double blind study since the levels of all the needed vitamins and minerals can be determined in the prospective mothers so that nutrients can be given for the production of better babies.

A double blind study is eventually analysed using statistical methods which require homogeneous populations of mice, rats or people. The schizophrenias are not homogeneous. If a double blind approach is not appropriate in unclassified diseases from fevers to the schizophrenias, what valid proof of efficiency can be applied? In 1943 we published a paper on caffeine withdrawal headache as a clinical entity by using the individual patient as his control. The patients abstaining from caffeine drinks of all kinds were given numbered envelopes which contained increasing doses of caffeine. On the seventh or eighth day all the capsules in the envelope were placebos which on withdrawal of caffeine precipitated a monstrous headache. The patient appeared at the laboratory, where the headache was studied biochemically and the patient was treated.

If biotypes of mental illness are studied biochemically and the observations are pertinent to the treatment of the biochemical imbalance, then the patient can be used as his own control by substitution of placebo capsules at any time after improvement of the patient. Blood or urine samples at the time of relapse confirm the original biochemical hypothesis. A series of such patients treated in the same fashion will satisfy the need for reliable proof of the existence of the syndrome and its treatment. This use of the patient as his own control occurs frequently as the patient runs out of nutrients and relapses into disperceptions and other symptoms of the original disease. Because nutrients improve the performance of the bodies' tissues, the placebo medication should be tried first.

In summary, the medicine of the future must not only conform to the rules of nature, avoiding the use of alien drugs where possible, but also conform to man's rules for ethics and objective science. Current scientific research often does not.

Guidelines for future research strategies

1. A double blind study with nutrients is often unethical and even criminal. For example, depriving a mother with a history of spina bifida of folic acid and other nutrients for the sake of a double blind study may cause deformed children.

2. Objective, measurable data provide hand-holes, the real keys to disease. The more reliance points, the more accurate the study. Why do a double blind study on B_{12} in pernicious anaemia when you can measure body status of B_{12}?

3. Double blind studies can only validly compare similar populations. The use of groups with similar ages and sex separation is not enough. We need similar biotypes according to the latest knowledge of the biochemistry of the disease. Schizophrenia is a complex of many biotypes. Behavioural classification is not enough to classify schizophrenia. More biochemical reliance points are needed.

4. Nutrient deficiency can be carefully assessed prior to any experimental trials or nutrient challenge tests and functional tests.

5. When a deficiency of a nutrient is established the response of

the patient to that nutrient is usually remarkable and also measurable biochemically. This gratifying response can be repeated by any open-minded investigator (and is the best test of a nutrient response).

6. A patient can be used as his own control to determine response, as we did in 1943 to establish caffeine withdrawal headache. The placebo trial should be given first.

7. The double blind test is best reserved for drugs in treating behavioural syndromes with no objective reliance points.

8. Other objections to the double blind test is the need previously to establish a fixed dose of the drug under test even if it is known that, for some individuals, a smaller dose is enough to produce the desired therapeutic effect. A four to tenfold spread may occur in the needed dose because of biochemical individuality. Another objection is the failure of correlation of day-to-day symptoms with drug or placebo effect. The observer does not know whether the patient is on drug or placebo so many casual observations may be lost. The human brain and senses are homed to a sharp peak of perfection in the true clinical investigator. Do not blindfold these individuals when they are studying nutrients. Instead, extend their senses with the known and useful biochemical tests for nutrients. These are blood and tissue levels, functional tests and preliminary challenge tests.

Finally, the reality of medicine is that 'only a minority of medical innovations are tested by a randomized controlled trial' (R. Taylor in *Medicine Out of Control: The Anatomy of a Malignant Technology*, Sun Books, Melbourne, Australia, 1979). In fact, a long list could be compiled of new therapies in the field of cancer chemotherapy alone that have been applied widely in practice as a result of clinical trials that did not involve randomization of patients.

Twenty-five thousand of our patients can vouch for the success of nutrition in treating their mental illness. And, in the end, this is what counts.

14

There is an Alternative to Hospitalization

Hospitals seldom follow the directions of orthomolecular practitioners. Thus intake of the essential nutrients is invariably stopped on entering psychiatric hospitals, and sometimes even for allergy testing. They think the patient may be allergic to the vitamins! Without the essential nutrients, which are known to be needed, the patient rapidly relapses and hospitalization is prolonged. Suitable alternatives to hospitalization must be provided or the patient may be shifted from allergy testing to the state psychiatric hospital for a long, slow recovery. The alternatives may range from halfway houses to treatment in the home under care of an operative nurse trained in the orthomolecular approach. Parents or relatives can also give orthomolecular care. The orthomolecular practitioner can thus continue to provide the medical care. This situation is similar to childbirth under the care of a wise midwife with the trained doctor available on call. The overall result is better and the patient will make continuous progress toward recovery from the cerebral allergy or mental disease.

The halfway house takes years of effort to establish. The usual population of patients at any one time will vary from six to twenty patients. Plans must be made for proper food, non-allergic housing, daily care and exercise and dismissal of patients. The houses will not make a profit so it should be organized as a not-for-profit unit and should receive help from government bodies or annual donations from benefactors. The insurance companies should pay for this care as they do for hospital care. Some voluntary help can be used to ease the great financial burden. Rosalind la Roche, who now runs Earth House in New Jersey, USA, was the first trained operative in the field of orthomolecular medicine. She heard, at a reception, of a recluse schizophrenic brother of a famous psychiatrist. She suggested that with her orthomolecular nutritional knowledge she could socially rehabilitate the recluse brother. She travelled halfway across America with packets of nutrients and within two months she had the recluse exercising daily and working at the family factory. He is now totally rehabilitated and is a member of the board of directors of Earth House. Such activity needs courage, strength, self-assurance and adequate training on the part of the orthomolecular operative. This training can be had at some of the orthomolecular centres around the world. Patients who cannot be left alone or patients who have withdrawn from society are the prime targets for therapy supervised by operatives.

Some drug crutches may be needed to get the patient in the mood for orthomolecular therapy. The orthomolecular operative is trained in the use of lithium (in small doses) and haloperidol drops which are tasteless and odourless. Haloperidol can thus be used covertly in the initial stages of therapy. As the patient gets better on the nutritional therapy, the dose of lithium and haloperidol can gradually be reduced. Dr Paul Janssen of Beerse, Belgium, once told me confidentially that he believed that half of the paranoid patients of Europe were on covert haloperidol treatment. The covert drops do work and we at the Brain Bio Center have had great success in the treatment of recluse, uncooperative schizophrenic patients. I usually place one drop of haloperidol on my tongue to demonstrate that the medicine is tasteless and odourless. The haloperidol liquid has been placed in milk, orange juice and in one instance under the plastic wrapper of frozen pizzas for the treatment of a paranoid boy who would not eat any of the food his mother cooked. He cooked and consumed the treated pizzas and got progressively better by the day!

As an alternative to the halfway house, a trained psychiatric nurse may agree to take a patient into her home for continued therapy. We have found this type of orthomolecular therapy to be highly successful and perhaps the least expensive of any arrangement. The new family milieu is particularly conducive to rehabilitation. It is obvious that any of these options are better than the psychiatric hospital or the rented bare apartment which is frequently suggested to get the patient away from the family. Premature isolation of the patient will result in malnutrition and the loneliness may lead to suicide.

15

Optimum Nutrition for Mental Health

Whether mentally ill or not, everybody can benefit from optimum nutrition. And the first place to start making changes is in your diet.

The ideal diet should contain as much as possible of the following foods: whole grains and wholegrain bread, fresh or dried fruits, wheat germ, sprouted seeds, legumes (such as lentils, peas, chick peas and beans), nuts, seeds, cheese, eggs, milk, brewers yeast, skimmed milk powder, seafood, poultry, organ meats and, occasionally, lean meats. In addition, safflower oil should be taken at the level of at least one teaspoon daily. Sunflower seeds can be eaten instead of the oil. The oil can be mixed with wheat germ and used as a morning cereal with milk and fruit.

The Brain Bio Center treats 'normal people' and patients from a metabolic nutritional viewpoint. The family physician can be in charge of normal nutrition and even simple preparations. But do avoid all mineral preparations with added copper! We do not recommend most commercial multivitamin and mineral tablets. These are usually loaded with copper which the whole population gains in excess from copper plumbing. We recommend distilled or bottled water if the house water supply is high in copper. Brass activated-carbon filters may actually add more copper to the drinking water. Softened water removes copper and substitutes sodium which is usually palatable but is bad for the high blood pressure patient.

Having said that, everybody can benefit from supplementing a healthy diet. The five key factors to consider are as follows:

1. Everybody needs enough B_6 for nightly dream recall.

2. Everybody needs a source of organic chromium such as is contained in brewer's yeast or chromium GTF tablets.

3. Everybody needs calcium and magnesium such as is contained in dolomite tablets.

3. Everybody needs an optimal dose of vitamin C which we estimate at approximately 2,000mg per day for an adult.

5. Everybody needs a dietary zinc supplement daily of about 15mg. Too much zinc produces a manganese deficiency.

The special supplement formulas most frequently needed according to age are:

Infants and Children

Children's Chewables made by Health+Plus
These contain 5mg of zinc, 1mg of manganese and 5mg of B_6 as well as all the other important vitamins and minerals – and no copper!
Infants up to the age of 1 can take two a day. Between the ages of 2 and 5, four a day is recommended. They can be sucked, or crushed and added to food.

Teenagers
Body growth and the hormone surge at puberty make great demands for adequate mineral intake. These demands are not met by junk food nor by standard vitamins plus minerals, which are too high in copper. Teenagers need:

VV Pack made by Health+Plus: One daily
This provides 75mg of B_6, 7.5mg of zinc, 1,250mg of vitamin C, 2.5mg of manganese and all the other important vitamins and minerals (except copper). Extra vitamin C and B_6, and zinc might also be needed as listed overleaf.

| *Vitamin C* | 1,000mg daily |
| *B₆, 100mg + Zinc, 10mg* | Enough for dream recall (but don't exceed 30mg zinc) |

These should be given if there are any signs of deficiency, which include frequent colds or infections, poor growth, white marks under the nails, acne, lack of periods or late sexual development.

Girls who are too tall for their age may need extra molybdenum which may help to control excess bone growth at puberty. Molybdenum can be obtained by eating lima beans, navy beans or wheat germ.

Adults
Adults, in addition to natural foods, usually need extra zinc, manganese and vitamin C. Tropical fruits can be used as a source of manganese. The following supplements are also recommended:

VV Pack made by Health+Plus	One daily
B₆, 100mg + Zinc 10mg made by Health+Plus	One daily
Vitamin C	1,000/2,000mg daily
Safflower or Sunflower oil	1 teaspoon
Dolomite	(if not drinking milk)
Vitamin A	25,000iu daily
Vitamin E	400iu daily

The Elderly
In addition to natural foods, vitamin C, zinc, B_6, other B vitamins, chromium, safflower oil and copper-free drinking water, the senior citizens have special needs. These are:

VV Pack made by Health+Plus	1, a.m.
B₁₂ + Folic Acid made by Health+Plus	2 tablets, a.m.
Dolomite + D made by Health+Plus	2 tablets, p.m.
Inositol, 200 mg	a.m. and p.m.
Choline, 250 mg	a.m. and p.m.

Selenium, 50 mcg   a.m. and p.m. (prevents
                                cancer and cataracts)
Molybdenum, 150 mcg   a.m. and p.m.

16

Nutrition Programmes for Specific Diseases

In addition to the basic dietary recommendations made in the previous chapter, we can make the following recommendations for people with specific diseases or one of the types of mental illness covered in earlier chapters.

Doses are given in mcg (1,000mcg = 1mg), mg (1,000mg = 1g) or g. All doses recommended are to be taken on a daily basis, with food, with the exception of amino acids. (Amino acids like tryptophan or methionine, are best absorbed on an empty stomach and if taken with fruit juice). These recommendations are best followed with supervision from your doctor or nutritionist, and neither the author nor the publisher can be liable for the effects of self-medication.

Optimum nutrition for mental illness

A. *Histapenia*
1. Niacin, 100mg and niacinamide 250–500mg
2. Folic acid, 1–3mg
3. Zinc (daily doses 10–30mg) and manganese (5–50mg), as gluconates
4. Vitamin C (2,000mg) to excrete copper
5. High-protein diet
6. L-Tryptophan, 500mg x 2 for sleep
7. B_{12} injection, weekly

B. *Histadelia, Allergy and Asthma*
   1. Calcium (as gluconate) 500mg, a.m. and p.m., to release histamine
   2. Zinc (10–30mg) and manganese (5–50mg) to build up basophils
   3. Methionine, 500mg a.m. and p.m. to excrete histamine

C. *Pyroluria*
   1. Vitamin B_6 (adequate for dream recall. Top dose = 2,000mg)
   2. Zinc (as gluconate) 30mg, a.m. and p.m.
   3. Manganese (as the gluconate) 10mg, a.m. and p.m.
   4. Plan to reduce tranquillizers if patient gets sleepy in daytime (Drug Flood Syndrome)
   5. If B_6 produces numbness of fingers or toes shift to pyridoxal phosphate at 1/10 dose.

D. *Depression*
   1. B_6 and zinc, a.m. (more B_6 up to dream recall)
   2. Zinc, 30mg, bedtime
   3. Deanol, 5 drops, each a.m. (available from Health + Plus)
   4. Vitamin C and Dolomite

E. *Senility*
   1. Deanol, 5 drops each a.m., or phosphatidyl-choline
   2. Magnesium, 600mg
   3. Vitamin C, 2,000mg
   4. B_6 + zinc (to dream recall)
   5. Manganese, 50mg
   6. Brewer's yeast and egg yolks, daily
   7. Weekly injection of vitamin B_{12}

F. *Childhood hyperactivity* (lead and copper intoxication)
   1. Vitamin B_6, adequate for dream recall
   2. Vitamin C, 100–200mg per day
   3. Zinc, 15mg and manganese, 10mg

4. Dietary restriction – no sugar or food additives
5. Deanol, 10 drops each a.m.

G. *Epilepsy*
1. B$_6$ to adequate dream recall
2. Vitamin C, 1,000mg, a.m. and p.m.
3. Manganese, 50mg, a.m. and p.m.
4. After 1 month: zinc, 15mg, at bedtime
5. Inositol, 500mg, 2 a.m. and 2 p.m.
6. Reduce anti-epilepsy drugs singly and slowly
7. Magnesium, 400mg, a.m. and p.m.

H. *Multiple Sclerosis* (50 per cent of patients may be pyroluric)
1. Safflower, sunflower or cod liver oil daily
2. B$_6$ to dream recall
3. Manganese, 50mg, p.m.
4. Lecithin capsules, 3 daily
5. Evening Primrose oil, 4 capsules daily

Optimum nutrition for skin problems

A. *Acne*
1. Biotin, 1mg, a.m. and p.m.
2. Zinc, 30mg, a.m. and p.m.
3. Manganese, 50mg, p.m.
4. Vitamin C, 1,000mg, a.m. and p.m.
5. Facial hygiene
6. Vitamin A, 25,000iu daily

B. *Psoriasis*
1. Lecithin granules, 1 teaspoon a.m. and p.m.
2. Evening Primrose oil, a.m. and p.m.
3. Zinc, 60mg, 2 daily
4. Manganese, 50mg, p.m.
5. Whole body sun beds
6. Vitamin C, 1,000mg, a.m. and p.m.
7. Vitamin A, 25,000iu daily

Optimum nutrition for metabolic disorders

A. *Arthritis*
1. Zinc (as gluconate), 30mg, a.m. and p.m.
2. Manganese (as gluconate), 50mg, p.m.
3. Vitamin B_6 to dream recall
4. Vitamin C, 1,000mg, a.m. and p.m.
5. Brewer's yeast, a.m. and p.m.
6. 2 egg yolks daily
7. Histidine, 500mg, a.m. and p.m.

B. *Hypoglycaemia* (zinc, manganese and chromium deficiency)
1. Avoid all refined sugars, alcohol and junk food
2. Zinc, 15mg, a.m. and p.m.
3. Manganese (as gluconate) 10mg, a.m. and p.m.
4. High vegetable-protein diet
5. Vitamin B_6 to dream recall
6. Vitamin C, 1,000mg, a.m. and p.m.
7. Chromium (GTF) daily
8. Regular exercise

C. *Diabetes*
1. Chromium GTF, a.m. and p.m.
2. No refined sugars
3. High vegetable-protein diet
4. Zinc, 30mg, a.m. and p.m.
5. Manganese, 50mg, p.m.
6. Vitamin B_6 to dream recall
7. Vitamin C, 1,000mg, a.m. and p.m.
8. Daily exercise

Hypertension (copper and cadmium intoxication)
1. Inositol, 500mg, 2 a.m. and 2 p.m.
2. Zinc, 30mg, a.m. and p.m.
3. Vitamin C, 1,000mg, a.m. and p.m.
4. High potassium-magnesium diet

   5. Vitamin B_6 to dream recall
   6. Low salt diet
   7. No manganese

E. *Heart Disease*
   1. Chromium GTF, a.m. and p.m.
   2. Magnesia tablets, 3 daily
   3. Low salt, high potassium diet
   4. Magnesium (as orotate), 400 mg, a.m. and p.m.
   5. Vitamin E, 400iu, a.m. and p.m.
   6. Zinc, 15mg, a.m. and p.m.
   7. Vitamin B_6 to dream recall
   8. Exercise daily to tolerance

F. *Arteriosclerosis*
   1. Vitamin C, 1,000mg, a.m. and p.m.
   2. Zinc (as gluconate), 30 mg, a.m. and p.m.
   3. Dolomite, 2 tablets a.m. and p.m.
   4. Vitamin B_6 to dream recall
   5. Daily exercise to tolerance
   6. Vitamin E, 400iu, a.m. and p.m.
   7. Daily fish diet or MaxEPA, a.m. and p.m.

G. *Migraine headaches*
   1. Zinc, 15mg as the gluconate
   2. Caffeine, each a.m. only (if addicted to coffee)
   3. Low salt, high calcium-potassium diet
   4. Magnesium (as orotate), 400 mg, a.m. and p.m.
   5. Vitamin B_6 to dream recall
   6. Vitamin B_{12} injection weekly or more frequently
   7. Fish daily

H. *Alcoholism*
   1. Join Alcoholics Anonymous
   2. Adequate vitamin B_6 for dream recall
   3. Methionine, 500mg, a.m. and p.m.

4. Calcium, 500mg (as carbonate), a.m. and p.m.
5. Vitamin C, 1,000mg, a.m. and p.m.
6. Extra B_1, B_2, B_3
7. Daily exercise

Optimum nutrition for pregnancy and fertility

A. *Pregnancy*
1. Bone meal, 2 tablets, a.m. and p.m.
2. Dolomite, 2 tablets, a.m. and p.m.
3. B_6 to dream recall
4. Zinc, 15mg, a.m.
5. Manganese, 5mg
6. B_{12} + folic acid, 1 tablet, each a.m.
7. Exercise daily

B. *Fertility*
1. Thyroid, 1 grain each a.m. (if needed)
2. Dolomite, 2 tablets, a.m. and p.m.
3. Zinc, 15mg, 1 tablet, a.m. and p.m.
4. B_6 to dream recall
5. Vitamin C, 1,000mg, a.m. and p.m.
6. B_{12} + folic acid, 1 tablet, each a.m.
7. Vitamin E, 400iu daily
8. Exercise daily

Optimum nutrition against cancer
1. Vitamin A, 25,000iu daily
2. Vitamin E, 400iu daily
3. Vitamin C, 10–20,000mg daily
4. B_6 to dream recall
5. Zinc, 15mg, a.m.
6. Manganese, 5mg
7. Selenium, 200mcg, a.m. and p.m.
8. Molybdenum, 500mcg, a.m. and p.m.
9. Glutathione, 100mg, or cysteine, 1g, a.m. and p.m.

10. Daily B_{12} injection a.m. and p.m.
11. No folic acid

Optimum nutrition for exercise

1. Chromium GTF, 3 tablets, a.m. and p.m.
2. Vitamin C, 1,000mg, a.m. and p.m.
3. Dolomite, 2 tablets
4. Vitamin E, 400iu, a.m.
5. Extra B_1, B_2 and B_3
6. Zinc (as gluconate), 15mg, a.m. and p.m.
7. Manganese, 10mg, a.m. and p.m.
8. Fresh fruit and vegetables; daily legumes

Optimum nutrition for insomnia

1. Zinc (as gluconate), 30mg
2. 2 dolomite, a.m. and p.m.
3. Vitamin C, 1,000mg
4. Inositol, 650mg, 1–2 tablets
5. Tryptophan, 500mg, 1–2 tablets
6. Lifestyle factors: sex, exercise, hot bath
7. 2 magnesia at bedtime

Optimum nutrition for obesity

1. Chromium GTF, 1 tablet a.m. and p.m.
2. B_6 to dream recall
3. Zinc (as gluconate), 15mg, a.m. and p.m.
4. Vitamin C 1,000mg, a.m. and p.m.
5. Niacin, 100mg, a.m. and p.m.
6. Carnitine, 500mg, a.m. and p.m.
7. Use salt substitute for potassium
8. Lifestyle factors: no evening snacks, no sugars, no salt. High vegetable-protein diet. Daily exercise of increased duration and intensity.

Conclusion:
Have Faith in Tomorrow's Medicine

Patients suffering from any type of chronic illness have probably already learned about the need for a generous supply of faith. They know the very large role that faith plays in all recovery.

Patients must have faith in themselves and in their own ability to combat an offending disease. Such crucial faith need not come from an evaluation of present assets. Honour and respect for the quality of life and the power to heal can stem from a focus on the sanctity of life itself, from a spiritual foundation or simply from an awareness of inner essence.

Because the therapist not only selects, but also directs treatment, much of the future lies in his or her hands. Faith in the therapist will lend support as he encourages and advises. Who else but the therapist searches the literature each night hoping to discover a new, improved treatment approach which is uniquely designed for the individual problems of each particular patient? Remember to have faith in the therapist, but do not allow blind faith. Be wary of catch–all diagnoses. A multiple sclerosis label is often placed on a zinc and vitamin B_6 deficiency. Alzheimer's disease labels frequently disguise simple aluminium poisoning and B_{12} deficiency. Because these distinctions suggest different therapies, an accurate diagnosis can be the key to a speedy recovery.

Have faith in the nutrients and medications given by the therapist. Do not lose confidence when weeks or months of therapy bring only minimal improvements or annoying side-effects. Instead, focus on the fact that it can take a long time to correct the serious biochemical and physiological imbalances which lie at the base of chronic disorders. Remember and be assured that one does not live this year with last year's body! All body tissues permeated by the circulation of blood and lymph can and will be influenced by better nutrition. Bones, muscles, and even the mind are constantly being replaced and made more efficient as proper nutrients and energy are supplied.

Medical and social science constantly progresses. By the time books are printed, they are often well behind the therapeutic knowledge published in journals. Faith in these journals, and the doctors and scientists who read and write the articles, has supported new knowledge, and as a result many disorders that were unmanageable ten years ago are now easily cured. As long as the future remains so thickly veiled, no man can predict what tomorrow will bring. Until such predictions are possible, faith in the continued progress of medical and social science will stand as a powerful personal resource. Believe in the future and the therapeutic rewards that come from research and study.

If, presently, a patient's syndrome cannot be allayed, remind them of the many people before them who have got well while combining faith in themselves with faith in the therapist, the treatment process, and the constant progress of scientific research.

Predictions for the Future

Here are some of my predictions for changes in nutritional therapy by the end of the century.

1. Zinc supplements of 15mg a day will be given regularly with manganese.

2. Manganese supplements will be larger – 25–30mg a day – and will be most useful in the treatment of allergy and depression.

3. Copper and aluminium will be more carefully eliminated from our drinking water.

4. Aluminium will be banned from water, foods, toothpaste and antacids.

5. Lead poisoning will be treated and prevented by the use of zinc and vitamin C.

6. Rubidium, cesium, strontium and lithium will find their places in nutrition as essential trace elements which are needed by man.

7. Molybdenum will be used to modulate excessive foetal growth in animals and man, and help easy births.

8. Cancer will be treated by proper nutrition, including manganese, zinc, selenium, molybdenum, vitamins E, A, C, and B_{12}, and cysteine.

9. A better standard 'table salt' with calcium, magnesium, potassium, selenium, zinc, manganese, and iodine will become available.

10. All centres for the mentally ill might use this salt plus vitamin B_6. No harm will be done and great good may ensue for some individual patients.

11. Mental health centres will have their own nutritional laboratories.

12. Branched chain amino acids will be used intravenously instead of glucose in hospitals.

13. Tyrosine and phenylalanine will be the treatment choice in depressed patients.

14. More trace elements may be found, such as boron for plants and iodine for animals. A great event was the dawn of speech in the porpoise and man. Perhaps a comparative study of speech areas of the brains of these two species may show involvement of a specific trace element.

Summary of the Schizophrenias

DIAGRAMATIC FLOW SHEET

Procedure:	Histapenia	Pyroluria	Histadelia	Cerebral allergy
History	No family history Hallucinations Paranoia Slow orgasm Many dental fillings Stalagmitic obesity	Family history Pallor White nails No breakfast Amenorrhea No dream recall Breath and body odour Abdominal pain Impotence Anaemia Poor dental enamel	Family history Suicidal depression Compulsions High pain sense Blank mind Good teeth Allergies Headaches	Family history Infantile eczema Coeliac disease Allergies Daily mood swings Relief with fasting
Lab Tests	High serum copper Low blood histamine High hair copper	High KP – urine High or low serum zinc High or low zinc in hair	High blood histamine Normal serum copper	Low blood histamine Rapid pulse Provocative testing Skin testing 4-Day elimination diets Food and symptoms diary 4-Day fast
Treatment	Niacin Folic Acid Vitamin B_{12} Pantothenate Zinc-manganese	Vitamin B_6 Zinc	Calcium Methionine Diphenylhydantoin Zinc-manganese	Eliminate antigen Vitamin B_6 Vitamin C Calcium Potassium
	40 per cent Histapenia	30 per cent Pyroluria	20 per cent Histadelia	10 per cent cerebral allergy

References and Further Reading

Since 1961 more than 200 papers have been published in leading journals throughout the world by the research team at the Brain Bio Center. The following books have also been published, all of which make excellent reading. These are:

The Schizophrenias: Yours and Mine, Dr Carl Pfeiffer (1980)
Mental and Elemental Nutrients, Dr Carl Pfeiffer, Keats (1975)
The Factbook on Zinc and Other Micronutrients, Dr Carl Pfeiffer (1978)
The Golden Pamphlet, Dr Karl Pfeiffer et al, Brain Bio Centre (1980)

Other books by Patrick Holford provide an excellent background to the new world of nutrition. These are:

The Whole Health Manual, Thorsons (1981)
Elemental Health, Thorsons (1983)
Detoxifying Lead and Other Heavy Metals, Institute for Optimum Nutrition (1984)
Vitamin Vitality, Collins (1984)

Also highly recommended is *Schizophrenia – A Fresh Approach* by Gwen Howe, published by David & Charles (1986).

A full list of the 178 scientific references, broken down by chapter, is available from the Institute for Optimum Nutrition, 5

Jerdan Place, London SW6 1BE. Please send a large SAE and £1 to cover photocopy charges.

The key references can also be found in the Institute's library which is open five days a week for ION members. Membership details are available on request.

Useful Addresses

Health+Plus are a vitamin company selling high-quality products with Dr Carl Pfeiffer's treatments in mind. For example, they do a multivitamin without folic acid for the histadelic. Write to Health+Plus, Health+Plus House, 118 Station Road, Chinnor, Oxon OX9 4EZ. Tel: 0844 52098.

Bio Lab is a laboratory that can run histamine and kryptopyrrole tests. Requests for testing must be referred by a doctor. Their address is The Stone House, 9 Weymouth Street, London W1N 3FF. Tel: 01-636 5959.

Institute for Optimum Nutrition has a nationwide network of nutritionists, trained in the orthomolecular approach. The Institute's magazine publishes a Directory of Nutritionists. This is available for 75p. Treatment is available at the Institute with Patrick Holford. Patients at the Institute also have access to all the tests mentioned in this book. ION also offers training for health professionals. Write to ION, 5 Jerdan Place, London SW6 1BE. Tel: 01 385 7984/8673.

Mind's full title is the Association for Mental Health and it is concerned with extending the services available to the mentally ill as well as providing support and advice. It also has a network of local support groups. The address is 22 Harley Street, London W1N 2ED. Tel: 01-637 0741.

National Schizophrenia Fellowship is a national organization for all matters concerning the relief of suffering of schizophrenics and their families. They specialize in promoting and supporting an excellent network of local self-help groups. Their address is 78 Victoria Road, Surbiton, Surrey KT6 4NS. Tel: 01-390 3651.

Richmond Fellowship for Community Mental Health is an international organization with forty-five therapeutic communities ranging from places that provide intensive rehabilitation programmes to group homes and day centres. They also run a Community Mental Health College for health professionals in the field and a consultative service for those wishing to set up similar homes. For more details contact 8 Addison Road, London W14 8DL. Tel: 01-603 6373.

Sanity is a voluntary organization that raises funds to further research into nutritional and biochemical factors in mental illness. Every penny goes towards research and it is well worth supporting. For details write to Mrs Marjory Hall, Robina, The Chase, Ashley, near Ringwood, Dorset BH24 2AN. Tel: 04254 79880.

The Schizophrenia Association of Great Britain was the first association in the U.K. for schizophrenia sufferers and their families. It is supporting a programme of research in the Biochemistry Department of the University College of Wales, Bangor. It aims to educate its membership about schizophrenia and to give them hope that schizophrenia will be conquered if adequate research in the right areas is done. The Association will need many volunteers, both patients and their near relatives, for participation in their research programme. If you can help or want more information about schizophrenia please write to: Gwynneth Hemmings, The Schizophrenia Association of Great Britain, International Schizophrenia Centre, Bryn Hyfryd, The Crescent, Bangor LL57 2AG, Gwynedd, Wales.

Index